FUEL FIGHT

the Florida battle over Orimulsion, Venezuela's "liquid coal"

Dale Andrew White

TWIN RIVERS PRESS
AMAZON.COM

Sources: Manatee Orimulsion Conversion Project 1994 Site Certification Application to the Florida Department of Environmental Protection; transcripts of the April 23, 1996, Sept. 9, 1997 and June 24, 1998 public hearings of the Florida Power Plant Siting Board; Sarasota Herald-Tribune, Bradenton Herald, Tampa Tribune, Tampa Bay Times, New York Times, Power-Grid.com, epa.gov, ScienceDirect.com, Electric Power Research Institute, Oil & Gas Journal, Energy Economist, S&P Global Market Intelligence, Energyintel.com, FPL.com.

Orimulsion.

Prior to 1993, few Floridians knew the brand name of an oil substitute that their state's largest electric utility wanted to be the first in the United States to import and burn.

Yet the word and its definition would gradually become widely known, making bold headlines and becoming the topic of kitchen table and government forum debates about the advantages and disadvantages of a hybrid power plant fuel often referred to as "liquid coal."

Florida Power & Light's pursuit of a state permit to retrofit one of its generating plants to use Orimulsion would become a costly, five-year legal battle that pit public officials against public officials and FPL against an expanding coalition of environmentalists, concerned citizens and corporate interests.

To understand the origins of this conflict, we must go back decades - before FPL sought approvals to build a power plant on an isolated, 9,500-acre site in Manatee County, on the west coast of Florida.

In 1969, Manatee adopted an air pollution code restricting fuel-burning installations, such as power plants and incinerators, from using fuels with more than 0.7 percent sulfur. Burning a sulfur-containing fuel produces sulfur dioxide (SO_2), a pollutant linked to acid rain and which the

American Lung Association says can be moved long distances by wind and cause respiratory ailments.

In 1972, while that ordinance remained in effect, FPL received local, state and federal approvals to construct a 1,600-megawatt plant (with twin 800-megawatt units) in Parrish, at the time a mostly rural hamlet of citrus groves, tomato farms, cattle ranches and multi-acre homesteads in northeast Manatee.

The utility would divert part of the flow of the Little Manatee River to create Lake Parrish, a 3,560-acre, private reservoir that would provide water for the plant's steam-generated turbines as well as coolant.

FPL chose to burn oil, even though a county ordinance limited that oil to 0.7 percent sulfur. The fuel would be brought by tanker to county-owned Port Manatee on Tampa Bay and then transported through a 16-inch, 14-mile underground pipeline to the generating plant.

Prior to the pipeline and power plant becoming operational, FPL argued that it should be allowed to burn less expensive, 1 percent sulfur oil at Parrish.

Persuaded by arguments of increased revenue for its fledgling seaport, the Manatee County Commission enacted an ordinance requiring FPL and any other industries to use fuel with a sulfur content no higher than 1 percent.

The first 800-megawatt unit commenced service on Oct. 26, 1976. The second unit did the same on Dec. 8, 1977.

Because 1 percent sulfur oil remained more expensive than other heavy fuel oils with higher sulfur content, FPL tended to use its Parrish generating plant at a third or less of its capacity.

So, by 1990, FPL expressed interest in a new product being promoted by Bitor America Corporation, a marketing arm of Venezuela's government-owned fossil fuel producer and exporter, Petroleos de Venezuela (PDVSA). The previous year, Bitor established an office in Boca Raton, Florida, and started contacting U.S. utilities about its new blended fuel that could be shipped and burned like oil but cost less: Orimulsion.

Beneath depleted oil fields in the Orinoco River region, PDVSA discovered extensive - and unusual - reserves of bitumen, a naturally occurring hydrocarbon in fossil fuel deposits. Unlike oil, these bitumen reserves were not liquid and could not as easily be pumped out. Unlike coal, the resources were not solid either and could not as easily be mined. This layer of a new fossil fuel source would be described as "tarlike" or similar to molasses.

"The problem has always been how to get this gunk out and sell it somewhere," Kim Fuad, an editor of Petroleum Intelligence Weekly, told the New York Times for a 1990 article about Venezuela's new "liquid coal."

Intevep S.A., the research arm of PDVSA, and British Petroleum's research affiliate developed a method of steam injection to extract this new energy source. Then it created a means of emulsifying it in water so it could become a liquid fuel.

PDVSA branded its new product "Orimulsion," a reference to the Orinoco River region and the fact that the fuel is an emulsion.

Venezuela estimated it could convert the extracted bitumen into an estimated 267 billion barrels of Orimulsion, which it could sell like oil but price like cheaper coal.

Researchers worked on testing and improving the product for the Bitor marketers to sell.

Prior to securing FPL's interest, PDVSA exported Orimulsion to utilities in Japan, England, Canada and Denmark. A consortium that included Texaco, General Electric, TECO (Tampa Electric Company) and Bitor America proposed an Orimulsion project in Yabucoa, Puerto Rico, but encountered public opposition.

British Petroleum initially had a 50 percent interest in BP Bitor, which marketed Orimulsion in Europe. Frustrated by the sparse interest in the product, in 1993 BP sold its half interest to

PDVSA, which renamed the marketing firm Bitor Europe.

Bitor America, however, had found a very interested potential customer in FPL.

"We have 11 plants that can be converted to Orimulsion," an FPL spokesman told the New York Times in 1990. He estimated that the utility could save $3 billion to $5 billion over 15 years. "... Orimulsion is a win-win situation. It's stored, transported and burned like oil, but priced like coal."

Yet there would be a snag if FPL were to switch from low sulfur oil to Orimulsion so it could use its Parrish plant at a desired 87 percent capacity. With 2.7 percent sulfur, Orimulsion would violate Manatee County's nearly two-decades-old, revised air pollution ordinance.

FPL executives thought that, if they made some concessions, they could convince the Manatee County Commission to revise the local law and support their effort to modify the Parrish plant's state permit.

Before taking that crucial step, they could benefit from having an ally among the politicians on the commission. They would find that ally on the ballot in the fall 1992 election.

***

John Gause, a retired FPL engineer and stockholder, resided in County Commission

District 1, which included Parrish. He became a candidate for the commission and got elected several months before FPL's Orimulsion plans became public.

During his re-election campaign four years later, Gause maintained that he had no advance knowledge of FPL's Orimulsion proposal when he took office. Regardless, as a commissioner, he became FPL's strongest advocate on the dais - often referring to his former employer in the first person as "we - the company."

FPL's critics argued that Gause should declare a conflict of interest because of his ties to the utility and abstain from voting on any matters regarding the Orimulsion project. Gause refused.

In June 1993, at the urging of FPL, the Manatee Commission voted 5-2 to lift the ban on burning oil with a sulfur content higher than 1 percent. Instead, local industries - such as FPL - could burn fuels with higher sulfur content if they used "emission control devices, fuel blending or other means" to limit SO_2 emissions to the same rate as 1 percent sulfur oil (1.1 pounds per million British thermal units of heat input). The commission majority also deleted the code's prohibition on coal.

In exchange, FPL promised lower electricity rates, more property tax revenue, new jobs associated with expanded use of the Parrish plant and more income for Port Manatee.

Approximately 120 citizens attended the public hearing. Of the 30 who stepped to the podium to speak, about half spoke in favor and half against.

Commissioners Gause, Stan Stephens, Patricia Glass, Lari Ann Harris and Maxine Hooper approved the new ordinance. Commissioners Kent Chetlain and Joe McClash cast the dissenting votes. McClash would become one of the most persistent and vocal critics of the Orimulsion proposal in the years ahead.

The change in local law cleared a path for FPL to seek other government approvals and prepare its application to the state for a permit to convert the Parrish plant from oil to Orimulsion.

***

In April 1994, contingent on its securing the state's approval, FPL signed a contract with Bitor for a 20-year supply of Orimulsion. It hoped to have its Parrish plant ready for the fuel change in 1998.

In August 1994, the Florida Public Service Commission - which authorizes electric utility rates - approved FPL's financial plan for the switch to Orimulsion and allowed FPL to use $72 million from the first year of fuel cost savings to reimburse itself for retrofitting the plant with pollution controls.

In September 1994, FPL submitted a detailed, six-volume application to the Florida Department of Environmental Protection explaining why and how it intended to become the first utility in the United States to import and burn a fuel state regulators knew little about. The DEP determined that the proposed changes at FPL's Manatee County operations were extensive enough that the utility must apply for a permit under Florida's Electrical Power Plant Siting Act as if it were seeking approval of a new generating station.

For six months, with the DEP channeling and tracking their questions to FPL and FPL's answers, several other entities would have input regarding the permit application including Manatee County, the Southwest Florida Water Management District and the Tampa Bay Regional Planning Council.

The filing of the permit application simultaneously started a case file with the Florida Division of Administrative Hearings. If the DEP, which initially considered the application "insufficient," eventually determined the submission to be complete and "sufficient," it and other agencies could submit their recommendations. The "sufficient" application and the various recommendations would then be the subject of a "certification hearing" by an administrative law judge.

The hearing would likely take several weeks.

After considering all the testimony and evidence, the administrative law judge would submit a written opinion of approval or denial to the Power Plant Siting Board, the members of which were the governor and Cabinet.

The Power Plant Siting Board would conduct its own public hearing about the Orimulsion project. By a unanimous or majority vote, Florida's highest elected officials - four Democrats (Gov. Lawton Chiles, Commissioner of Agriculture Bob Crawford, Treasurer Bill Nelson and Attorney General Bob Butterworth) and three Republicans (Secretary of State Sandra Mortham, Comptroller Bob Milligan and Commissioner of Education Frank Brogan) would decide whether Venezuela's controversial "liquid coal" would have a future in the Sunshine State.

***

Orimulsion consisted of roughly 70 percent bitumen, more than 29 percent fresh water and less than 1 percent of an emulsifying agent. (The latter would become a major source of contention.)

Another breakdown showed Orimulsion to be 60 percent carbon, 7.5 percent hydrogen, 0.5 percent nitrogen, 0.2 percent oxygen and 2.7 percent sulfur (and possibly as high as 2.9 percent sulfur) - plus the water and emulsifier. Like other fossil fuels, Orimulsion contained traces of sodium, nickel, beryllium, arsenic, fluorides and lead. It was reported to be low in mercury but high in vanadium.

FPL stated that Orimulsion has "no single molecular formula" because the formula can change and had changed as recently as 1993 because of the emulsifying additive.

As of the permit application, the primary additive, at 0.17 percent, was nonylphenol ethoxylate, a surfactant that caused the bitumen to become suspended in water. PDVSA added magnesium nitrate, FPL stated, "to help stabilize the emulsion and counteract high temperature corrosion in the (power plant) boiler."

FPL explained to state regulators that Orimulsion would reduce its systemwide dependence on oil from 35 million gallons a year to 14 million gallons. The new fuel would also "displace approximately 87,000 gigawatt hours of oil generation over the 20-year life of the project, saving approximately 135 million barrels of oil."

FPL stressed that its industry must be prepared for change, such as deregulation and an era when consumers could chose their electricity providers. It needed to be able to compete with utilities that used the cheapest fossil fuel, coal.

The utility's agreement with Bitor tied Orimulsion to the price of coal. The price of fuels for power plants is based on heat content, not volume. At the time, FPL tended to pay $1.56 per million British thermal units for coal, $2.02 for 3 percent sulfur oil and, for the 1 percent sulfur oil burned at Parrish, $2.22. "In the unlikely event that coal prices exceeded those of oil or gas, the price of Orimulsion will be capped by the lowest priced fuel," the company informed the DEP.

For consumers, FPL projected a net savings of approximately $6 billion over 20 years or, for a typical household, $42 a year.

FPL also touted the local economic benefits of its Orimulsion project: an annual increase in revenues for Port Manatee of more than $1.5 million; retrofitting the Parrish plant would create approximately 350 construction jobs; 40 new jobs would be created because of new air pollution controls and an additional 50 jobs associated with the transportation of limestone and recyclable products to or from that air quality equipment.

If the conversion to Orimulsion did not happen, FPL warned, it could consider closing the Parrish plant, which employed about 120 and then paid about $1 million in annual property taxes.

***

When addressing the possible environment impacts of its Orimulsion project, FPL acknowledged that the question of whether an Orimulsion spill could occur in Tampa Bay loomed large.

Oil spills had occurred before in the water

body flanked by Manatee, Hillsborough and Pinellas counties.

The most recent happened in August 1993, when a phosphate freighter and two barges collided. One barge, which was supposed to deliver jet fuel, diesel fuel and gasoline to the Port of Tampa in Hillsborough, caught fire. The other barge, loaded with fuel oil for FPL's Parrish plant, spilled its cargo, which formed a 10-mile-long oil slick.

In its application to the DEP, FPL specified the precautions to be taken with the 110 deliveries of Orimulsion it expected to receive yearly at its Port Manatee terminal, each shipment being the equivalent of 250,000 to 300,000 barrels.

Bitor America would use double-hulled tankers preferably no more than 10 years old. Cargo holds would have an empty chamber between each chamber containing Orimulsion to divert the fuel should a leak occur.

At Port Manatee, Orimulsion would be unloaded at a rate of 10,000 to 20,000 barrels an hour through two 10-inch hoses. An "apron" beneath each hose and a containment boom between the ship and the dock would be in place to capture any accidental spillage.

Yet, if a spill occurred in Tampa Bay despite all of the precautions, the fact that Orimulsion would not form a slick like oil remained troubling.

FPL acknowledged that, in a spill, the fuel "ceases being Orimulsion and becomes a particulate bitumen suspension in seawater."

Clarence Troxell, a Parrish retiree who would later establish a local citizens group to oppose the Orimulsion project, described the potential consequences more simply: "In case of a tanker spill, it would be like trying to get Ovaltine out of milk."

FPL informed the DEP that the University of Miami was working on a "damage assessment" using computer models of how Orimulsion could disperse in Tampa Bay. Meanwhile, the DEP would review tests of a simulated spill at Cape Canaveral Marine Services to determine the effectiveness of a combination of meshes, booms and skimmers in retrieving bitumen.

Setting the recovery issue temporarily aside, FPL assured state regulators that Orimulsion would be no more toxic to marine and plant life than the oil it was already importing - an assurance that environmentalists would still consider unacceptable.

***

At FPL's Port Manatee Terminal, Orimulsion would be pumped into two insulated steel tanks that could contain a 12-day supply. From there, it could be pumped through the existing pipeline to the power plant.

The pipeline's monitoring system could detect a minimum leak of 50 barrels but could be upgraded to detect a leak of 25. Through a quarter-inch puncture, the fuel could leak at a rate of 1.3 barrels per minute. With upgrades, the monitoring system could detect a leak in 20 minutes. Computers could stop pumps, close valves and shut down the pipeline within three minutes.

FPL did not expect "increased internal corrosion" because of Orimulsion's water content. Like oil, Orimulsion would form a thin coating of hydrocarbon to protect the pipeline's inner metal walls.

***

In 1991, FPL tested Orimulsion at its 400-megawatt plant at Sanford and confirmed it could be used in burners designed for oil. The retrofitting of the Parrish plant would mainly involve the installation of emission controls between the burners and the smokestacks so the new fuel would not exceed already established air pollution rates.

Under its existing permit for 1 percent sulfur oil, the Parrish plant could emit up to 0.1 pounds per million Btus (British thermal units) of particulate matter (primarily ash or soot), 1.1 pounds of sulfur dioxide, a pollutant linked to acid rain, and 0.3 pounds of nitrogen oxide.

All combustion processes, including motor vehicles, produce nitrogen oxide (Nox). Nitrogen oxide is a strong oxidizing agent and plays a major role in the atmospheric reactions with volatile organic compounds (VOC) that produce ozone (smog). NOx causes the yellowish-brown haze associated with smog. The nitric acid in ozone breaks down into hydrogen and nitrate ions, contributing to the "acid rain" that feeds algae blooms and kills fish.

When it enters the atmosphere, NOx converts into nitrogen dioxide - which health authorities say aggravates heart diseases, respiratory diseases and pulmonary diseases and, in animal studies, is linked to damage of the liver, spleen and immune system.

The Tampa Bay National Estuary Program cited NOx as a major cause of seagrass loss and other deterioration in that water body.

The Sanford tests showed that, without emission controls, Orimulsion would emit 0.128 to 0.215 pounds of particulates, 4.15 to 4.23 pounds of SO_2 and 0.46 to 0.58 pounds of NOx per million Btus.

Pure Air - a partnership of Air Products & Chemicals Inc. and Mitsubishi Heavy Industries based in Allentown, Pennsylvania - would own, install and operate the pollution controls.

A $45 million electrostatic precipitator (ESP) would create a high-voltage electric field in which negatively charged particles would be removed from the flue gas. Pure Air anticipated 90 percent efficiency, reducing the emission rate for particulates to .03 pounds per million Btus.

Pure Air projected that $135 million flue gas desulfurization scrubbers (FGD) with wet, crushed limestone would be 95 percent efficient and reduce SO_2 emissions to 0.234 to 0.3 pounds per million Btus.

The ESP and FGD were also expected to remove about 90 percent of beryllium, 50 percent of mercury, 90 percent of fluorides and 50 percent of arsenic from the flue gas.

Yet the pollution controls would produce waste and by-products for which Pure Air and FPL would have to make disposal arrangements.

***

The scrubber system would produce 710,000 dry tons annually of gypsum, a sulfate mineral. Pure Air proposed selling the gypsum to wallboard and cement manufacturers.

The ESP would produce from 19,800 to 22,000 dry tons annually of flyash to be sold to the cement industry,

Approximately 202 round trips of truck traffic each day would deliver limestone for the FGD scrubbers and remove the gypsum and flyash. If the byproducts could not be sold, FPL proposed dredging and filling wetlands on site for a landfill.

***

FPL stressed that, because of the pollution

controls, the maximum annual tonnages of all regulated pollutants would be less than maximums allowed under its existing permit, about 77,768 tons lower.

Yet, because the Parrish plant tended to be used at 30 to 33 percent of its capacity, it had not come close to emitting the 83,351 tons of SO2, 9,442 tons of particulates or 22,732 tons of NOx allowed annually under that current permit.

However, the Department of Environmental Protection wanted comparisons with "actual" or "historical" emissions rather than permitted maximums that were not occurring. By its staff analysis, total emissions of regulated and unregulated pollutants could increase by 81 percent.

The DEP especially expressed concerns about NOx, saying those emissions could increase from an average of 7,294 tons per year to 17,491 tons.

FPL countered that, when burning Orimulsion, the Parrish plant would displace power otherwise generated at the Sanford, Cape Canaveral, Fort Myers, Port Everglades and Turkey Point plants, which used 3 percent sulfur oil. While NOx emissions at Parrish could increase by 10,000 tons annually, NOx emissions from the other five plants would decline by 24,000 tons - yielding a "net systemwide decrease of 14,000 tons per year."

As it does with new power plants, the state

could insist on "best available control technology." For NOx emissions, that technology could be selective catalytic reduction (SCR). The state required SCR when authorizing new coal-burning power plants to achieve a NOx emission rate of 0.17 pounds per million Btus compared with the 0.3 pounds rate that FPL intended to maintain at Parrish.

In SCR, ammonia is injected into the flue gas. NOx and ammonia mix, then pass through a "catalyst" made of materials such as titanium dioxide, vanadium pentoxide and tungsten trioxide. A reaction occurs, breaking down the NOx and ammonia into nitrogen and water.

Instead, FPL proposed spending $5 million on low-NOx burners, which are designed to control fuel and air mixing to reduce peak flame temperature and NOx formation. That approach would minimize the gas during the combustion process instead of with "backend cleanup" technology.

FPL also argued that SCR could add $42 million in annual costs to a project in which the utility expected a total investment of $72 million. The expensive catalyst, which lasts eight or more years in plants burning other fuels, might have to be replaced every two years if used with Orimulsion. Plus SCR would require more truck traffic for the large amounts of ammonia and disposal of the metallic catalyst.

***

In May 1995, the DEP concluded that FPL's permit application was at last "sufficient" - complete and comprehensive enough for the agency to prepare its recommendation to the administrative law judge.

ManaSota-88, an environmental group in Manatee and neighboring Sarasota County, had already filed to be a party in the upcoming proceedings.

Launched in 1968, the organization started as an environmental health study by the U.S. Public Health Service, Florida State University, University of Florida and the Sarasota and Manatee County Commissions with a 20-year span outlook.

At some point, it evolved into an independent non-profit of local activists and their donors and supporters taking firm stances on bi-county issues such as sewage sludge, toxic pesticides, wetlands protections, urban sprawl and especially phosphate mining.

To the unsuspecting, ManaSota-88 Chairwoman Gloria Rains appeared as harmless and apolitical as a short, white-haired, cookie-baking grandmother. Yet in her countless battles with developers, polluters and the politicians they supported, Rains became a fireball. She consistently made sure ManaSota-88's strategy did not change: Do not negotiate. Do not compromise.

That no-compromise approach caused ManaSota-88 to lose many battles in County Commission and other chambers. Yet it also solidified the organization's reputation for sticking to its principles.

As soon as she learned of the specifics in FPL's Orimulsion plan, the Manatee County resident consulted with ManaSota-88 attorney Thomas Reese to start building a case for its defeat.

At the same time, a retiree in Parrish - who would become a determined ally of Rains - would learn about FPL's Orimulsion project and develop his own concerns.

Three years prior, Clarence Troxell retired as general manager of transmission and distribution for Public Service Electric and Gas of New Jersey. He and his wife moved to River Wilderness, a golf course subdivision in Parrish on the north shore of the Manatee River - six miles southwest of FPL's power plant. His attorney daughter, Amy Stein, and her husband would also relocate from New Jersey and purchase a home in the same neighborhood.

Troxell, who earned a degree in electrical engineering from Yale University and a master's in the same from Stevens Institute of Technology, read a newspaper account about FPL's interest in Orimulsion.

`"I asked my friends up north," Troxell later

told the Sarasota Herald-Tribune. "They had been approached by Bitor ... and my own company had turned it down because of environmental reasons."

If Troxell presumed his retirement years would be a relaxing blend of golf, warm winters and Gulf coast sunsets, he willingly postponed that lifestyle to take on an almost full-time avocation of studying FPL's Orimulsion proposal and, at personal time and expense, building his own battle plan.

Like Rains, Troxell would not compromise either.

Both tenacious, determined and unrelenting, Rains and Troxell would become the public faces of a citizens-led insurrection against the Orimulsion project - even though they realized FPL's political influence and monetary muscle would likely stack the odds heavily against them.

***

After the DEP accepted FPL's permit application, other entities gradually started registering their opinions.

The Tampa Bay Regional Planning Council, which includes representatives from local governments in six counties, addresses growth related and other issues of mutual interest. In July 1995, the TBRPC gave conditional approval for the Orimulsion project with its two members from the Manatee County Commission, Gause and freshman commissioner Gwen Brown, joining in the decision. Yet the affirmative nod came with several stipulations: FPL should use selective catalytic reduction technology to keep NOx emissions at the current level. The utility should be required to participate in prevention efforts regarding a potential tanker spill and retrieval of the dispersed bitumen and restoration of Tampa Bay should a spill occur. The regional council also wanted proof that increased withdrawals from the Little Manatee River, with headwaters in Hillsborough County, would not adversely affect the river and its ecosystem.

The TBRPC asked if natural gas would be a better option, as many environmentalists contended, because FPL had switched from oil to gas elsewhere in its system. Yet FPL noted that the closest natural gas pipeline to its Parrish plant was 90 miles away.

In August, in a private meeting, the Manatee County Commission voted 6-0 to also give its conditional consent. Commissioner McClash, a vocal critic of Orimulsion, was on vacation and did not attend.

Commission Chairman Stan Stephens explained that, since the state had the ultimate say, the commissioners preferred to negotiate stipulations with FPL. Those stipulations required air pollution controls but did not include SCR, participation in spill prevention and recovery efforts should a spill occur, limiting truck trips to 404 a day with a limit of 10 per hour during morning school zone and school bus route hours and assurances that increased withdrawals would not negatively impact the Little Manatee River.

In September, the governing board of the Southwest Florida Water Management District expressed concerns about air quality and a potential spill in Tampa Bay for DEP to address. Yet its unanimous opinion primarily focused on preventing FPL from diverting more water from the Little Manatee River than the 7 million gallons a day it was already taking (less than 10 percent of the river's flow). FPL initially suggested increasing withdrawals to up to 16 million gallons a day.

The water management district urged FPL to instead use groundwater wells and recycled wastewater. The Manatee County Commission would later promise to work with FPL on getting 7.7 million gallons of recycled wastewater from its sewage system to the Parrish plant each day and another 4.3 million gallons of groundwater per day.

Before the month ended, in preparation for the administrative hearing slated to begin Nov. 28, the DEP released its long-anticipated decision. The state's environmental regulators supported FPL's switch from oil to Orimulsion. Yet their report included 100 pages of conditions regarding spill prevention, air pollution controls, use of recycled wastewater and other precautions, as well as a $5 million penalty plus recovery costs if a spill occurred in Tampa Bay.

***

Across the Atlantic Ocean, environmentalists became aware of FPL's Orimulsion plans and regarded the specifics to be very familiar.

"There are certainly similarities with events here in Wales," Gordon James, head of campaigns and development for the Cardiff chapter of Friends of the Earth, told the Sarasota Herald-Tribune.

Friends of the Earth opposed National Power's plan to switch its 2,000-megawatt, 28-year-old plant at Pembroke, Wales, from oil to Orimulsion - expressing the same concerns as FPL's opposition.

A month or so prior to FPL's administrative hearing, ManaSota-88 and Friends of the Earth acknowledged that they were sharing information and advice.

In 1991, National Power applied for a government permit to burn Orimulsion at a plant it was using at just 14 percent capacity. The utility cited the same benefits as FPL: consumer savings, construction jobs, increased use of an expensive capital asset.

That application, James contended, "was a disgraceful attempt to get away with the very minimum of pollution controls."

As did Florida's DEP regarding FPL's Parrish plant, Her Majesty's Inspectorate of Pollution determined that the modifications at Pembroke needed to burn Orimulsion were extensive enough that National Power would have to go through the same permitting process required for a new generating station.

Parliament member Frank Dobson, the Labor Party's "shadow" for the Secretary of State for Energy, labeled Orimulsion "the world's dirtiest fuel." Local and regional governments, such as the Countryside Council of Wales, warned that NOx and SO2 pollution would reach excessive levels.

Because of the unfavorable political climate, National Power withdrew its initial proposal and filed a modified plan. That second application included electrostatic precipitators to trap particulates, flue gas desulfurization to reduce SO2 and low-NOx burners.

In Wales, as in Florida, government agencies and political leaders became divided about the merits of National Power's updated plan.

Her Majesty's Inspectorate of Pollution recommended approval by Michael Heseltine, a member of Parliament who served as Secretary of State for Energy. The South Pembrokeshire District Council and the Dyfred County Council dropped their opposition. Pembroke's member of Parliament

(MP), Nick Ainger, favored the project. Yet MP Alan Williams of nearby Carmarthen and MP Denzil Davies of nearby Llanelli opposed it.

Although FPL wanted to be the first U.S. utility to use Orimulsion, National Power did not have that distinction in the United Kingdom.

In 1992, PowerGen received approval to use the hybrid fuel at its 360-megawatt Richborough plant near Sandwich on the Kent coast and its similar size Ince plant in Merseyside - with no emission controls.

In March 1995, Prudential, the insurance company, sued PowerGen because of alleged pollution from the Richborough plant. Prudential owned an 800-acre vegetable farm about a half mile away. The company and its tenant farmer argued that air pollution damaged the farm's sprouts, greens and lettuce.

In October, PowerGen announced it would shut down the Kent plant.

***

A few weeks before the administrative hearing, Troxell publicly challenged FPL's calculations that the fuel switch would save consumers $3.50 per month or $42 annually. At a forum about the Orimulsion issue, he contended the savings may more likely be 50 cents per month or $6 per year.

FPL countered that the $3.50 figure given the

Public Service Commission was an average over 20 years.

Contacted by the Herald-Tribune, the assistant director of the PSC's Division of Electric and Gas said FPL's "savings claims" were "checked for reasonableness" but not verified for absolute accuracy. The agency stated that the consumer savings would likely start at 82 cents per month in 1998, climb to $3.97 by 2009 and level off at $3.57 in 2017.

FPL presumed that low-sulfur oil would cost $3.11 per million Btus in 1998 and, over 20 years, rise to $9.40. The utility forecasted Orimulsion as costing $1.53 per million Btus in 1998 and rising to $2.89 by 2017.

Yet the PSC staff stated that they did not concur with FPL that the cost difference between oil and Orimulsion would appreciatively widen over 20 years.

At the time, FPL customers paid a monthly fuel charge (on which the utility was prohibited from making a profit) of 0.01747 cents per kilowatt hour. Yet, even if that rate declined with Orimulsion added to the utility's energy mix of oil, coal, gas and nuclear, PSC regulators could adjust other charges unrelated to fuel expenses. So, a household's total bill could increase despite the lower kilowatt hour charge for fuel.

***

During a three-week span that started after Thanksgiving 1995, Administrative Law Judge J. Lawrence Johnston presided over a hearing in Manatee County's convention center in which FPL presented its case about the economic and environmental benefits of switching its 19-year-old power plant several miles to the northeast from oil to Orimulsion.

Thomas Reese, an attorney for ManaSota-88 and Manatee County Save Our Bays, represented the opposition.

After closing arguments, Johnston spent several weeks reviewing the evidence and more than 2,400 transcript pages of testimony by 30 witnesses for FPL and another dozen summoned by the environmental groups.

In January 1996, the DEP released its recommendation that the governor and Cabinet approve the importation and use of Orimulsion with the stipulations agreed to by FPL.

FPL's opposition focused their wrath on DEP Secretary Virginia Wetherell, accusing her of evidently overruling the concerns of the agency's lower-ranking employees. Their suspicions intensified when they learned that FPL had hired her husband, former House Speaker T. K. Wetherell, as a lobbyist and that the Tallahassee law firm representing the company in the Orimulsion case hired her stepson.

FPL and the Wetherells denied any connection between the hirings and DEP's recommendation in favor of Orimulsion.

In February, Johnston issued a lengthy ruling that also urged the Power Plant Siting Board to give FPL its seven thumbs up, establishing dozens of "findings of fact" in support of the utility's plan.

Johnston concluded that the Orimulsion Conversion Project would lessen air pollution, substantially reduce the chances of a tanker spill in Tampa Bay and not inflict a truck traffic burden on Parrish's roads. He saw no definitive proof that the emulsifier in Orimulsion, commonly called phenol, could act as a female hormone and harm the reproduction of marine life. He accepted FPL's estimates about fuel cost savings, consumer savings and increases in local jobs, tax revenue and Port Manatee revenue. Because of the expense and disposal concerns, he disagreed with the suggestion that FPL should be required to install selective catalytic reduction to reduce NOx emissions. He did not foresee increased withdrawals from the Little Manatee River as being an issue, especially if FPL worked with Manatee County to primarily use wells and recycled wastewater.

"The Project serves and protects the broad interests of the public," Johnston wrote.

He dismissed arguments offered by Reese and his witnesses as "novel theories" that "have no merit," even as "unintelligible" or "not supported by any evidence."

Reese expressed hope that he could still convince a majority on the Power Plant Siting Board to reject the Orimulsion project and all the agency recommendations in its favor. "I don't think it's a done deal," he told the Herald-Tribune.

Although not a "done deal," if Gov. Chiles and Cabinet members gave greater weight to Johnston's opinion and all of the testimony, evidence and recommendations he considered valid than they did the arguments to be repeated by the anti-Orimulsion faction, FPL's struggling opposition had to admit that their odds of prevailing against the state's largest utility did not appear favorable.

In March, just weeks before the Power Plant Siting Board would conduct its hearing, their cause suffered another blow. The U.S. Environmental Protection Agency, which initially expressed numerous concerns, decided that the Orimulsion project met applicable federal regulations. Its OK would allow the U.S. Army Corps of Engineers to issue a dredge and fill permit should FPL need an on-site landfill to dispose of any unmarketable ash and gypsum.

***

On April 23, 1996, Gov. Chiles and the six Cabinet members convened in the state Capitol in

Tallahassee as the Power Plant Siting Board.

They faced a packed chamber with more than 200 witnesses and spectators (dozens of whom arrived from Manatee County on a chartered bus), with an overflow crowd in a hallway watching the proceedings on a monitor.

The politicians heard representatives of FPL, Bitor America and Pure Air provide an overview of the proposed new permit for the Parrish plant.

FPL senior vice-president C.O. Woody emphasized, aside from the $42 in projected annual savings for a typical household using 1,000 kilowatt hours per month, the fuel switch could save a large industrial customer as much as $1 million a year and taxpayer-supported institutions, including public schools, a collective $12.9 million.

Given the cost savings, spill prevention precautions and pollution controls, approval of the conversion project was "environmentally the right thing to do, as well as economically the right thing to do," Woody said.

Others stepped forward to express their support.

An assistant professor of marine biology and fisheries from the University of Miami said an "apples to apples" comparison of the effects of oil and Orimulsion in case of a spill showed the latter to be "no less acceptable" than the fuel FPL was already importing into Tampa Bay.

A retired U.S. Coast Guard captain with experience in oil spill containment said Bitor America "committed to operational practices that are far in excess of those that are required or that are currently in use by the maritime industry today." He regarded the proposed shipments of Orimulsion to be "about eight times safer" than the oil tankers already coming into Port Manatee.

Stressing that he was not an FPL stockholder, an airline pilot from Manatee County said that "my environmental friends" expressing concerns about the effect of increased NOx air emissions on Tampa Bay should "instead focus on some of the communities up and down the coast that are poisoning our bays and rivers." He specifically mentioned the Manatee County city of Palmetto, which released its treated wastewater containing nitrogen into Terra Ceia Bay, which connects with Tampa Bay; the county seat of Bradenton, which released treated wastewater into the Manatee River, a tributary of Tampa Bay; and Sarasota County, which contended with septic tank pollution into its bay waters.

A Methodist minister who served as president and CEO of Goodwill Industries in Sarasota-Manatee praised FPL as "a good corporate neighbor" and stressed that lower electricity bills would especially help low-income families.

The director of a cement supplier at Port

Manatee said his company could use the gypsum by-product from the scrubbers to be installed at the Parrish plant.

A 23-year resident of Parrish whose family owned a 1,000-acre cattle ranch expressed confidence in FPL's research and expertise. "I have no problem as a resident of Parrish with the Orimulsion project," she stressed.

The chairwoman and chief executive of Schroeder-Manatee Ranch, a 27,000-acre agricultural enterprise flanking the Sarasota-Manatee border that was gradually converting its property into the residential development Lakewood Ranch, said there are no absolute guarantees that an accident will not occur. "Airplanes fall out of the sky. Locomotives run into each other." Yet society has not banned airplanes and trains, she said.

The business manager for a union representing FPL's electrical workers urged approval "for the sake of our careers and the sake of the environment and the cost of the customers."

***

St. Petersburg Mayor David Fischer stepped forward as the first speaker opposing Orimulsion. He emphasized that his city features "the largest municipal shoreline in the state of Florida," 124 miles. "We have never been consulted on this issue."

Since being admitted into the National Estuary Program in 1990, Tampa Bay experienced gradual recovery in water quality and seagrasses after decades of degradation, Fischer said. He did not want to see that progress stop.

Manatee County Commissioner Joe McClash said the executive committees of that county's Democrat and Republican parties both opposed Orimulsion, making such opposition a bipartisan issue.

McClash noted that, though use of the county's recycled wastewater is a condition included in the proposed permit, no agreement between the county and FPL had been made yet. "A pipeline has to be built."

He reiterated concerns about a tanker spill. Orimulsion "disperses into the whole water column, turning it black from top to bottom, especially in the shallow waters of Tampa Bay."

McClash referred to the Siting Board as "the safety net for the people in the state of Florida." If the panel approved Orimulsion at Parrish, its use would expand across the state, he warned.

Manatee County Commissioner Lari Ann Harris confirmed the board on which she served declined to support or oppose FPL's permit application and instead secured an agreement with the utility for various concessions if it got state approval. Yet she stressed that NOx and SO2 emissions from the Parrish plant could legally triple if FPL increased use of the oil-fired facility to meet demand. Regarding a potential tanker spill, rather than ban the shipment of any fuel, Harris said the state should "require as many precautions and safeguards as possible."

Approval or denial of the permit application "does, in fact, come down to new technology versus the status quo," Harris said.

Thomas Reese, attorney for ManaSota-88 and Manatee County Save Our Bays, told the Siting Board it was about to make "a major policy decision, not only for the state of Florida but for the United States."

If the Parrish facility were yet to be built, the state would require "best available control technology," Reese said. For NOx emissions, that technology would be selective catalytic reduction. SCR in combination with low-NOx burners would cost $4,000 for every ton of NOx removed, he added. "And we do not believe $4,000 is economically prohibitive."

He regarded 400 daily truck trips through Parrish as "totally unacceptable."

Bitor's plan to use booms with 10-foot skirts to retrieve an Orimulsion spill would not be effective in Tampa Bay's 40-foot-deep channel, Reese argued. "And the channel actually acts like a pipeline. The water moves through that channel at very rapid rates. It would disperse the area."

Amy Stein, Troxell's daughter, appeared as the spokesperson for three homeowner associations in the River Wilderness subdivision. She and others were "appalled" by the "deficiencies in the record and the recommended order (from the administrative law judge) that the project should be approved."

Johnston determined that an increase in local air pollution was justified by "alleged reductions outside Manatee County," Stein said. She added that "pollution in the Tampa Bay area doesn't respect political boundaries."

Stein noted that the effects of a potential Orimulsion spill had been analyzed in "only experimental test spills" in tanks, such as what DEP described as a "bathtub test" with a simulated spill at Cape Canaveral in a tank with a diameter of 26 feet and depth of four feet. "Nowhere ever in the world has an Orimulsion spill been contained or cleaned up in open waters."

Stein wondered how much of the phenol used to create the emulsion of bitumen and water "is going to escape into the atmosphere" when burned. (In its later rebuttal, FPL contended that the surfactant would combust at 425 to 450 degrees and that the boilers would exceed 2,000 degrees.)

She called the consumer cost savings cited by FPL as "very speculative and questionable."

Quoting the costs per kilowatt hour for coal and oil in 1995, she argued that the monthly consumer savings on the fuel portion of that typical household bill would be closer to 90 cents rather than $3.50 and would be initially further reduced to pay for plant conversion expenses.

Stein listed more than two dozen organizations and entities that opposed Orimulsion, including several that would follow her in the public hearing as well as the Tampa Bay Agency on Bay Management, Sarasota Bay National Estuary Citizens Advisory Committee, Parrish Civic Association, North River Republican Club of Manatee County, Federation of Manatee County Community Associations and the coastal municipalities of Sarasota, Longboat Key, Anna Maria and Holmes Beach.

One by one, spokespeople for the Legal Environmental Assistance Foundation, Florida and Manatee-Sarasota chapters of the Sierra Club, Florida Wildlife Federation, Florida Consumer Action Network, Port Tampa Civic Association (the neighborhood through which trucks would deliver gypsum to a wallboard manufacturer), Manatee-Sarasota Fish & Game Association, Audubon Society and Florida Consumer Action Network - as well as several citizens speaking as individuals - stepped to the microphone to express concerns about spill risks, NOx emissions, truck traffic and other details.

Orimulsion "poses too many uncertainties," the spokeswoman for the Legal Environmental Assistance Foundation said. "And it basically uses Florida's human and environmental resources as guinea pigs."

***

In a closing argument, an attorney for FPL reminded the state's highest elected officials that they were to give "meaningful consideration and due weight" to the opinion of the administrative law judge, which featured 258 "findings of fact" based on 200 exhibits and 50 witnesses (who gave 2,600 pages of testimony) at the certification hearing.

All of the benefits for the fuel switch cited by his client were "amply supported by competent substantial evidence" and were "a result of the most far-ranging studies for a power plant project ever conducted in this state."

Agriculture Commissioner Crawford proposed adding several conditions to the permit including: taking steps to "offset" the "nitrogen loading" into Tampa Bay by the same amount that could be attributable to the plant's NOx emissions; limiting daily truck traffic to 145 round trips; requiring FPL or Pure Air to pay $500,000 "up front" for road improvements and $25,000 annually to a trust fund to benefit the Parrish and Port

Tampa communities; and a future update to the Siting Board on FPL's compliance with all conditions in the new permit.

He then made a motion for approval, which Secretary of State Mortham seconded.

Governor Chiles acknowledged that the DEP and administrative law judge "worked long and hard" to reach their recommendations. "We sit in a different capacity," he said of the Siting Board. "We sit to decide public policy."

He doubted that, "at this stage," Florida's power industry, which had been expanding its use of natural gas, needed an additional fuel. Although Orimulsion could eventually be accepted in the United States, "I'm not sure Florida should rush to be the first to use it. ... I'm just not ready for my vote to roll the dice on this one and to take a chance of how this would come down."

Attorney General Butterworth made a "substitute motion" to instead deny the application. Treasurer Nelson seconded it. In a roll call vote, they and Comptroller Milligan supported the denial. Mortham, Crawford and Education Commissioner Brogan voted "no."

Chiles delivered the deciding vote: "Yes."

As the governor adjourned the meeting, the 4-3 decision reportedly left FPL executives and supporters stunned and slack jawed. Having regarded themselves as a slingshot-armed David taking on a deep-pocketed, corporate Goliath, the opposition factions expressed surprise as well before bursting into cheers and uninhibited elation.

Yet neither side could be sure who would be the ultimate winner or loser. The political and legal fight over Orimulsion would soon prove to be far from over.

Three weeks later, FPL filed a lawsuit asking Florida's First District Court of Appeal to overturn the Siting Board's decision.

***

The night before the Siting Board vote, Rains confidently - and confidentially - correctly predicted to a newspaper reporter the 4-3 decision and which politicians would vote yes and no.

The environmentalists and other citizen activists spent months, not just picketing outside hearings but giving media interviews to broaden public awareness of their cause. They spearheaded letter-writing campaigns to the Siting Board members and secured roughly 9,000 signatures on petitions, plus 147 postcards that the Sierra Club distributed at an Earth Day event.

Bob Hite, the news anchor for the NBC-TV affiliate in Tampa, aired a demonstration using Tampa Bay waters of how spilled oil formed a floating slick and Orimulsion dispersed throughout another sample. Troxell played that video for the Siting Board and its audience.

The week before the Siting Board meeting, ManaSota-88 and others conferred with the top aides of the governor and Cabinet members to reinforce the details of their opposition. Those sessions gave them a clue as to which direction each elected official appeared likely to sway.

The narrow, preliminary victory convinced Rains that her no-compromise strategy proved to be the correct approach.

It also altered the political landscape in Manatee County in an election year.

Stein already filed to run against Gause for the Republican nomination in County Commission District 1. So did another opponent of the Orimulsion project.

In the September primary, none of the District 1 candidates prevailed. Stein led with 46 percent, followed by Gause with 30 percent. Gause and Stein would be on the ballot again for an October runoff.

Gause received the endorsement of the Manatee Chamber of Commerce's political action committee, which financed polling for his campaign. Stein secured the support of the Sierra Club and many Parrish residents, including members of the North River Republican Club.

Stein won the Republican nomination with 67 percent. Gause blamed the media for his loss, saying it distorted his environmental record.

In November, Stein handily beat a Democrat challenger with 68 percent of the vote. For at least the next four years, District 1 would be represented by a commissioner committed to defeating FPL's Orimulsion ambitions.

In the Republican primary, Commissioner Maxine Hooper found herself challenged by a political newcomer as well. Jonathan Bruce, an owner and manager of rental properties, disagreed with the incumbent's vote to eliminate the local ban on high-sulfur fuels and allow FPL to proceed with its state permit application. Bruce defeated the citrus grove owner with 54.2 percent of the vote. With no Democrat or write-in candidate in that race, Bruce would become the next commissioner to represent District 5, which spanned the southeast sector of the county.

McClash, a landlord and owner of a plumbing, heating and air conditioning business, initially faced an opponent. Yet his challenger withdrew after the candidate qualifying period ended in July. McClash, who won re-election as an at-large representative of the entire county, would no longer be the lone dissenter on the County Commission regarding the divisive Orimulsion issue. He would gain two allies on the seven-member board when they took the oath of office in November.

Stan Stephens, a builder backed by the

Chamber of Commerce, faced two challengers in the Republican primary for the District 3 seat representing a western sector of the county that included the beaches: the owner of a swimwear shop in the commercial fishing village of Cortez and a meter repairman for Manatee County Public Works, both of whom criticized the incumbent's environmental positions.

Stephens barely prevailed with 51.2 percent.

Jane von Hahmann, the retailer, placed second with 34.4 percent. In a rebuttal to the Bradenton Herald's endorsement of Stephens, she had linked the incumbent with a commission majority willing to "compromise" the quality of the region's air and water.

Four years later, von Hahmann ousted Stephens for the Republican nomination with 3,187 ballots to his 2,089. She won the general election by a landslide against a write-in candidate who did not campaign.

***

In May 1997, FPL made a presentation to the Manatee County Commission about changes it intended to make to its Orimulsion plans to address the "quality of life" issues that the public evidently considered to be of greater importance than fuel cost reduction on their monthly bills.

The utility now claimed it could cap NOx emissions at "historic levels," about 7,318 tons per year, while also increasing use of the Parrish plant. FPL previously expected to keep the NOx emissions rate at 0.3 pounds per million Btus. It now told commissioners that new burners could reduce NOx by controlling the amounts of fuel and oxygen to create a flame. The emissions rate could drop to 0.16 pounds per million Btus, slightly lower than the 0.17 pounds that the DEP and environmentalists cited as possible with more expensive SCR technology.

Under FPL's revised plan, with increases in carbon monoxide but reductions in sulfur dioxide and the amounts of NOx, volatile organic compounds and particulate matter remaining the same, annual tonnage of overall air emissions could decline by 18 percent.

An Orimulsion spill test conducted off the coast of Venezuela by Bitor America showed a bitumen recovery rate of 82 percent, FPL told the county commissioners. Should their case be remanded back to the Siting Board, Bitor and FPL would explain how that result got achieved.

The 202 round truck trips for limestone deliveries and removal of emission controls residue that residents of Parrish considered objectionable could be reduced to 30 by mostly using railcars, FPL said. Yet the utility would have to also pay for the construction of train platforms for loading and unloading.

The utility offered to use some of the cost savings that otherwise would go to its customers for other benefits.

In exchange for state approval of Orimulsion, FPL and Bitor would donate $1 million for a vessel tracking system for Tampa Bay's seaports. FPL would also donate $200 million over 20 years for a trust fund for "projects and research" by nonprofit organizations to benefit Tampa Bay's environment. That fund would be overseen by a board with a representative of FPL and representatives of area county governments, the Siting Board, the Area Agency on Bay Management, Tampa Bay Regional Planning Council and other entities. The utility also promised to donate an initial $1 million, plus $25,000 annually, for a community trust fund to benefit Parrish.

***

The next day, the First District Court of Appeal decided it was not ready to confirm or deny the Siting Board's rejection of FPL's Orimulsion permit.

A three-judge panel agreed that the Siting Board must have "rejected" at least some of the administrative law judge's 258 "findings of fact." It remanded the case back to the governor and Cabinet to "delineate with specificity" which findings they considered to be in error.

ManaSota-88 hoped the Siting Board would

not reopen the entire case but merely go through the "findings of fact" and identify which the majority of members found troubling or questionable.

"The information is all there," Rains said. "It's just a matter of citing the pages and paragraphs - bing, bing, bing."

Yet FPL regarded another opportunity before the Siting Board as "a second chance" to secure its consent by introducing its proposed changes to its original application, none of which were considered by the administrative law judge, Public Service Commission or other entities that had a previous say in the matter.

***

By early June, FPL released the video it previously touted as showing successful Orimulsion spill recovery demonstrations done in Venezuela.

The tests were conducted for Petroleos de Venezuela and requested by the Florida DEP, which said the "bathtub tests" done in tanks "didn't represent real-world situations."

The nine-minute video showed two demonstrations, "dockside" and "offshore."

The dockside test simulated what could happen if a hose broke while Orimulsion was being unloaded at Port Manatee. About 10 gallons of Orimulsion was "spilled" into the berth's waters, where equipment was already in place to recover it. In that scenario, about 94 percent of the bitumen got retrieved.

About 15 kilometers offshore, a crew dumped about 100 gallons of green dye into the Caribbean Sea. The crew learned they would need 150 feet of floating boom to encircle the spill. The boom would be the same as that used for oil recovery but with an attachment, a submerged, 9-foot-long skirt. The video showed no visible amount of dye getting past the boom or skirt.

Workers then used 150 feet of skirted boom to create an enclosed circle in which they poured 100 gallons of Orimulsion. Footage shot by divers showed the bitumen particles dispersing in the seawater but not escaping past the skirt.

A "forced adhesion and flotation system" blew air into the submerged cloud of bitumen and water, which stripped the bitumen of its emulsifying agent. Clumps of bitumen were then skimmed off the water's surface and pulled aboard a vessel with a conveyor belt.

In the open-water test, 82 percent of the bitumen got recovered.

A U.S. Coast Guard captain who witnessed the experiments claimed to be "impressed" by the results. An emergency response official for the DEP who also attended the tests acknowledged that a 94 percent recovery for a spill at a seaport berth may be possible. Yet he said the open-water test was done under "ideal conditions," with spill containment crews and equipment already in place.

To further back up its claims, FPL cited an analysis by a marine consulting and spill management firm in Massachusetts.

Those consultants claimed that, with FPL's current fuel shipments to Port Manatee, a 1-in-200 year chance of an oil spill occurring in Tampa existed. Yet with the double-hulled tankers and other precautions promised by Bitor, the chance of an Orimulsion spill would be 1-in-796 years.

As expected, FPL's critics in the Tampa Bay region remained critical of the video recording and the new data.

"It was not an open-water spill," Troxell said of the video. "It was a very controlled spill. The Orimulsion was poured from the top. That's not the same as a break in the hull. It wasn't influenced by current or tides or anything."

"What happens when it floats out of the (shipping) channel" before the skirted boom can be in place? Rains asked. "Parts of the bay are just 3 feet deep. All the marine organisms in the water column will be killed or damaged."

***

By the summer of 1997, Petroleos de Venezuela shipped Orimulsion to utilities in five nations, with contracts to sell more than 5 million metric tons of the unique fuel annually.

New Brunswick Electric Power in Canada received up to 800,000 tons per year for its Dalhousie Power Station.

SK Power in Denmark, which previously backed out of a deal for undisclosed reasons but reconsidered, had recently committed to 1 million tons per year for its Asnaes Power Station.

Lithuanian Satat Power Systems got 500,000 tons a year for its Electranai Power Station.

In Japan, three energy companies relied on Orimulsion. Kashima Kita Electric Power Corporation bought 355,000 tons per year for its Kashima Power Station. Mitsubishi Chemical wanted 300,000 tons annually for its Mitsushima Power Station. Kansai Electric Power expected to burn 200,000 tons per year at its Osaka Power Station.

The People's Republic of China became the seventh Orimulsion customer. North China Power Group ordered 1 million metric tons of the oil substitute for its Dagang Power Station.

Bitor set a goal of selling 15 to 20 million metric tons of Orimulsion annually by 2002. So far, the distributor was at about a third or fourth of the way toward reaching that benchmark.

According to Energy Economist, an industry journal, Bitor's original projections were to sell 12 million metric tons annually by 1992. Five years later, total sales were less than half that.

Bitor initially targeted Ireland, Spain and Portugal as potential markets and could not get utilities in those nations to commit. The loss of PowerGen in the United Kingdom came as a setback, as did the project in Puerto Rico. And, because of environmentalists' vocal opposition, the pending deal with National Power in Wales for 4 million tons would be in jeopardy.

Bitor would be courting other potential customers in Italy, Germany and Thailand. Yet it needed a confirmation of the pending 20-year contract for 4 million metric tons per year with FPL to greatly boost its global marketing efforts. And the fate of that deal again rested with a panel of politicians sensitive to the opinions of the statewide electorate.

***

In June 1997, David and Casey Gluckman, a prominent husband-and-wife attorney team known for championing environmental causes to the Florida Legislature, made the surprising announcement that they accepted FPL as a client and supported its Orimulsion case.

The lawyers - known for representing organizations such as the Florida Wildlife Federation and the Save the Manatee Club - declined to disclose how much FPL paid them for three weeks of research that resulted in their 17-

page position paper in which they rated the pros and cons of the revised Orimulsion project.

David Gluckman admitted that, had FPL not made changes to its original plan, the duo with a combined 50 years of legal experience in environmental issues, may not have reached the conclusion that a shift from oil to Orimulsion would have "a net environmental benefit."

The Gluckmans rated the proposed overall air pollution measures (which would keep NOx levels steady and reduce sulfur dioxide even though carbon monoxide would increase) as "a significant plus." They reached the same conclusion regarding double-hulled tankers and other spill precautions and the proposed trust funds for Parrish and Tampa Bay.

Also getting the "significant plus" ranking were the proposed use of recycled wastewater to limit withdrawals from the Little Manatee River and a proposed wetlands mitigation strategy if a landfill at the Parrish plant would be needed. In exchange for disturbing 18 acres of wetlands for the disposal site, FPL would preserve 129 acres of wetlands along the river and create conservation easements on other sensitive properties it owned in the region.

The Gluckmans offered a "neutral" opinion on how booms and other equipment could retrieve spilled bitumen, calling the recovery assurances "too theoretical."

Regarding a comparison of the impacts of an oil or Orimulsion spill, the Gluckmans wrote: "Both fuels will have adverse but different effects on Tampa Bay. One is as bad as the other."

Overall, they concluded that, compared with oil, Orimulsion offered "a net environmental benefit."

Opponents of the Orimulsion project were not swayed. They referred to the Gluckmans as being "for sale" and their position paper as paid-for testimony.

Sticking with a "no compromises" strategy, Rains of ManaSota-88 faulted the Gluckmans' comparison of oil and Orimulsion. "I don't see that approach as pertinent. It's not a proper presumption that FPL must use either oil or Orimulsion - when the best fuel policy would be natural gas."

David Gluckman said he and his wife expected accusations that their findings must be tainted but insisted they were not influenced by who paid for their report. "We're not selling anything to anybody. We point out what we think is the truth."

***

About two months prior to the Siting Board meeting to discuss its response to the appellate court, FPL released additional evidence that it wanted the elected officials to consider.

On behalf of Bitor America, the University of Massachusetts at Amherst conducted a year-long study regarding whether the emulsifying additive phenol (nonylphenol ethoxylate) causes sexual disorders and deformities in fish and wildlife.

Although Proctor & Gamble and Lever-Pond stopped using phenol in their products, other manufacturers continued to include it in laundry detergents, stain removers, household cleaners and other products that go down drains, through sewage treatment plants and possibly into water bodies, which might also receive phenol from fertilizer runoff.

Phenol contains xenoestrogens, which mimic the female hormone estrogen, and endocrine disruptors. Orimulsion's critics said phenol might be linked to penile malformations in alligators, hermaphroditic organs in fish and other gender-bending malformations - as well as declining sperm counts and testicular and prostate cancers in male humans.

The United Kingdom had already banned phenol from household detergents. Its environmental agency warned Bitor that Orimulsion might not be approved in Wales if it continued to contain phenol. Denmark took a similar stance, saying SK Power would have to discontinue using the fuel if the emulsifying agent had not been changed by the end of 1998.

On Bitor's behalf, the university researchers and an environmental sciences lab in Jupiter Beach, Florida, tested Intan-100, the brand of phenol that accounted for 0.22 percent of Orimulsion. They exposed sheepshead minnows to varying quantities of the product.

The minnows that were exposed to high amounts of phenol for several weeks experienced reproductive difficulties and had fewer offspring. However, trials that duplicated phenol levels from an Orimulsion spill reportedly indicated that the chemical would become diluted and degraded by bacteria and other organisms - causing no long-term negative effects on marine life.

Orimulsion opponents dismissed the Bitor-financed report as conflicting with other environmental scientists' global concerns about phenol as a pollutant.

Troxell, who went to Wales the previous month to confer with environmentalists and politicians there and form a pact called the Florida-Wales Alliance for Clean Air, said that 0.22 percent may not sound like a significant amount of the additive. Yet he stressed that the 8.8 billion pounds of Orimulsion that could be shipped through Tampa Bay would include almost 20 million pounds of phenol.

Whether the governor and Cabinet would hear arguments for and against the University of

Massachusetts report would depend on whether they strictly elaborated on their previous 4-3 decision based on the record, as the appellate court asked, or allowed new evidence in the case.

***

Several weeks before the Siting Board session, FPL representatives escorted a contingent including two newspaper reporters, a Tampa City Council member, the president of the Parrish Civic Association, representatives of the Florida Audubon Society and other observers to Dalhousie, New Brunswick, Canada.

The government-owned New Brunswick Power solved an air pollution problem there by converting its 100-megawatt generating station on Chaleur Bay from coal to Orimulsion. NB Power executives, the mayor and town manager and local residents praised the switch that occurred three years earlier - with good reason.

Winters in Dalhousie, at last, became white again.

The power plant, built in 1969 on the town's waterfront, initially included a coal storage yard. That eyesore was now gone. So was the soot that coated clotheslines and anything left outside. "Every fresh snowfall would be covered in black soot," the town manager remembered.

Compared with the local coal, which could have a sulfur content as high as 8 percent, the

Orimulsion brought in twice a month in double-hulled tankers seemed to be an improvement - especially since retrofitting the plant included adding scrubbers to reduce sulfur dioxide emissions and an electrostatic precipitator to capture ash containing heavy metals. The gypsum from the scrubbers would be trucked to a nearby wallboard manufacturer and the ash to a steel manufacturer in Ohio.

Yet NB Power's $264 million Orimulsion project got off to a rough start.

In September 1994, just weeks after the change from coal to Orimulsion, a fan that pushes air into a boiler failed. Without enough oxygen, an incomplete combustion of fuel occurred . A black plume of unburned carbon shot up from a smokestack and rained specks across a third of the municipality, including the town manager's swimming pool.

NB Power spent about $300,000 for materials, labor and cash settlements to quickly make amends - repainting at least three homes, cleaning yards and washing houses and cars.

A representative from Bitor America told the Florida delegation that the accident was not related to Orimulsion and would have happened with either coal or oil.

Regardless, that soot incident did not get repeated. The first power plant outside of Europe and Asia to commit to Orimulsion resumed functioning precisely as planned.

The conversion project so impressed editors at McGraw-Hill's trade magazine, Power, that they bestowed the publication's 1995 Powerplant of the Year Award on the Dalhousie generating station for "leadership in the application of fresh ideas" and raved about the design and technology.

Yet the visitors from Florida made town officials start to wonder aloud about NB Power's use of the Venezuelan import.

"All this discussion about Orimulsion, we're surprised at it," Mayor Wally Coulombe told the group. "People told me: 'You know, we're getting bad press in Florida.' I said: 'What the heck have we done to Florida?' I don't like bad press about our town if it's not the truth."

The mayor noted that the town, provincial and national governments were investing $3 million to diversify the local economy beyond the paper mill, chlorine mill, power plant and commercial fishing industry by creating a recreational vehicle park with an indoor swimming pool to attract tourists.

"If we had (industrial) plants polluting here, that couldn't happen," Coulombe said of his community of 5,000 residents. "You can't have soot showering down on tourists."

***

A month prior to the Siting Board's much-anticipated next session, FPL launched a print, radio and television advertising campaign to promote its Orimulsion project.

Environmentalists, politicians and consumer advocates in Tampa Bay counties served by electric utilities other than FPL reacted negatively to the media blitz. They realized they would not have any customer benefits from FPL's new fuel choice but would be exposed to all the spill and pollution risks.

To raise awareness, about 25 demonstrators staged a protest at bayside Ballast Point Park in Tampa that attracted news reporters as well as observers from FPL and Bitor. While pickets waved signs with slogans including "Clean Air is Priceless," "Burn Now, Pay Later" and "Reject Fuel from Hell," a research team from Mote Marine Laboratory in Sarasota announced that CSX Transportation, the railroad FPL needed to use as an alternative to trucks, paid an undisclosed amount for them to study existing documentation about Orimulsion.

A senior scientist at Mote, a retired Coast Guard expert on marine safety, an aquatic toxicologist and a civil engineer who specialized in modeling oil spills spent 10 days reviewing what was already known about the hybrid fuel before releasing a seven-page report about their findings.

They commended Bitor by committing to take delivery precautions such as double-hulled tankers, tug escorts and a requirement of three-mile visibility before entering Tampa Bay. Yet they were unconvinced that "an ability to successfully contain or recover an Orimulsion spill has been adequately demonstrated." They suggested that the research on minnows that indicated minimal risk to marine life should be conducted on other species, such as scallops. They also noted that the spill recovery experiments conducted for FPL or Bitor were done "under static conditions and simulated or calm sea conditions" and offered no proof of effectiveness in a "large scale, open-water test."

A vice president of Bitor America responded by emphasizing the railroad monopoly financed the Mote report because it did not want to be required to assist FPL. Bitor claimed the Jacksonville-based company's concerns had nothing to do with environmental protection but with its regarding Orimulsion as a potential threat to its coal-hauling contracts with other utilities.

Regardless, the protestors welcomed CSX's decision to join their opposition forces.

Aside from spokespersons from Mote, the Florida Consumer Action Network and the Sierra Club of Pinellas and Pasco counties, several politicians stepped forward to tell Tampa Bay media why the public needed to tell the Siting

Board to stick to its previous decision and keep Orimulsion out of Florida.

"Life is all about acceptable risk," State Rep. Mary Brennan, a Democrat from Pinellas Park, said. "And Orimulsion is not an acceptable risk."

State Sen. Charlie Crist, a Republican from St. Petersburg who would become governor several years later, called for a statewide ban on Orimulsion until the Legislature could be convinced of the fuel's safety.

"I don't feel we should be guinea pigs in this area," St. Petersburg City Councilman Jay Lasita said. (A week later, in a 5-1 decision, that City Council approved a resolution opposing Orimulsion to be forwarded to the Siting Board.)

FPL representatives passed out a document to reporters suggesting they should ask questions such as: "How many lobbyists has CSX hired to oppose Orimulsion?" and "How much does CSX make from its coal operations?"

No one from CSX, which received the Mote report the day before, attended the event.

The Mote research team countered that CSX "paid normal rates" for "an independent review" of all public documents pertaining to the proposed shipment of Orimulsion and did not influence their conclusions.

***

The Florida-Wales Alliance for Clean Air,

the group Troxell helped forge, learned that Denmark imposed strict regulations on SK Power for workers exposed to Orimulsion. SK Power provided them with details, including photos of employees wearing masks and protective suits.

Troxell cited the information as evidence that Orimulsion ash must be especially hazardous.

An SK Power employee manual warned: "When exposing oneself to fly ash for a longer period (than the company allowed for various tasks) it might cause lung cancer, sinus cancer and skin allergy."

What protective suit an SK Power employee wore when retrieving or disposing of Orimulsion residue depended on that person's job - such as cleaning, welding or washing. Standard equipment could include a rubber suit, rubber gloves (with cotton gloves underneath), rubber boots, a face shield, a breathing filter and a ventilator. Time limits were imposed for some duties. A shower and a change of clothes were mandatory. The rubber suits were then vacuum cleaned, then put in water soluble bags and sent to the power plant's laundry.

SK Power told the Florida-Wales group it had encountered one employee with a health problem associated with the ash removal. A laundry worker mistakenly took ash handlers' protective suits out of the washing bags and developed an allergic rash.

FPL countered that power plant employees

should not inhale ash from any fossil fuel. When workers at its oil and coal-fired plants cleaned ash from boilers, they were required to wear masks for respiratory protection and overalls. Yet the utility acknowledged that Denmark's regulations were more stringent than those of the U.S. Occupational Safety and Health Administration.

***

On Sept. 9, 1997, another over-capacity crowd (including opponents who arrived by chartered bus) attended the Siting Board hearing to again discuss FPL's Orimulsion project.

An attorney for the utility insisted that the administrative law judge based his 258 "findings of fact" on "competent, substantial evidence." He admitted his client "misjudged the power of confusion" and erred by not adequately communicating the benefits of the fuel conversion - "cleaner air, a safer bay and lower electricity costs for 7 million Floridians" - to the general public. Instead, an opposition emerged that succumbed to "fear of the unknown and fear of change."

In response to that opposition, FPL said it proposed new conditions that it was willing to abide by voluntarily even if the Siting Board did not include the stipulations in its approval - such as trust funds for Parrish and Tampa Bay, the use of railcars and reduction in truck traffic, use of recycled wastewater for coolant and even lower

NOx emissions than previously projected.

With the added conditions, "the result will be less pollution in the state, less dependence on Mideastern oil, a cleaner and safer Tampa Bay and lower energy prices," FPL President Paul Evanson told the panel of politicians. "And I think, in the end, this equates to increased competitiveness for Florida businesses, more jobs and a better quality of life for all of our citizens."

The commanding officer for the U.S. Coast Guard's Marine Safety Office in Tampa testified that all the precautions proposed for shipments of Orimulsion "go beyond the existing regulations" and would make it "almost impossible" for any spill to occur in Tampa Bay. A former Coast Guard director of marine environmental safety programs concurred, adding that even with the increase in fuel deliveries, the spill risk of a tanker with Orimulsion would be "at least four times lower" than the tankers currently bringing oil into Port Manatee.

The executive director of the Tampa Bay Regional Planning Council said the updated spill prevention and recovery plan - which included Bitor's agreement to take out $1.2 billion in pollution liability insurance and FPL's $1 million commitment toward a vessel tracking system for area seaports - would be "the most complete and conscientious plan in the nation, if not the world."

All of the guarantees state, regional and local entities secured from FPL and Bitor for the Tampa Bay area will be lost if "another community that is less environmentally sensitive than ours will set the standard" for importing and burning Orimulsion, she warned.

An associate director of Florida State University's Center for Biomedical and Toxicological Research said an overall decrease in air pollutants would result in "a human health benefit."

The director of the University of Miami's Center for Marine and Environmental Analyses said more than 40 scientists from several universities and research institutions examined the proposed "risk management measures" and concluded that "the net total risk to the environment of Tampa Bay would be significantly reduced" if FPL made all the changes it agreed to include in its certification approval.

Dalhousie Mayor Wally Coloumbe said his Canadian town wants to protect its "healthy, year-round, deep seaport" as well as build a reputation as a tourist destination and would not allow Orimulsion if those priorities were endangered. "I can assure you our experience with Orimulsion has been a good one. ... Bitor America has kept its word and lived up to its commitments and, in my view, surpassed them."

***

Manatee County Commissioner Amy Stein stepped forward as the first speaker during the opposition's allotted time. She warned the Siting Board that if it approved "a very dirty, experimental and problematic fuel," other applications for Orimulsion will follow. Utilities could be committed to long-term contracts during an upcoming period "when renewable energy technologies become economically competitive." She stressed that her District 1 constituents overwhelmingly opposed FPL's plans, as evidenced by her defeating the incumbent by nearly 70 percent.

Stein showed a video by the NBC affiliated reporter Bob Hite about an experiment conducted by the Pinellas Seabird Rehabilitation Center, which specialized in cleaning spilled oil off birds. The staff poured Orimulsion into aquariums filled with sand and living sea grasses. The fuel reportedly dispersed in the water but also formed a coating on the surface and on the sea grasses. To determine its effect on birds, the researchers dipped a deceased seagull in a tank. They determined that Orimulsion was more difficult to remove from feathers than oil and more likely to get in creatures' eyes.

A spokeswoman for the rehab center later spoke to the Siting Board to express additional concerns. If manatees eat contaminated seagrasses, fish ingest contaminated water through their gills and birds eat contaminated fish, the devastating effects on wildlife could be widespread, she warned.

During FPL's later rebuttal, the president of the non-profit Ecological Research and Development Group claimed "the tape demonstrating the inability to clean impacted wildlife is simply wrong. ... Bottom line, we have effective tools to remove Orimulsion from avian feather structures, just as we do for any other heavy fuel product or weathered product."

County Commissioner Joe McClash criticized FPL advertising that referred to Orimulsion as "the fuel of the 21st century." He called it "the tar that nobody wanted in this century."

McClash compared FPL's claims about Orimulsion's safety with the claims about the Titanic that proved to be false and disastrous.

"We have not tested this product in a real-life situation," the commissioner said. He doubted the skirted boom would be effective in Tampa Bay's currents. "It's like the drapes in your house when the wind blows."

County Commissioner Jon Bruce stressed that his District 5 constituents in southeast Manatee also opposed Orimulsion. He joined Commissioners Stein and McClash in wanting to pass a commission resolution against the fuel switch but "kept getting shot down 4 to 3."

Bruce emphasized that "nowhere in the world is Orimulsion being used in the quantities that are being proposed for the Parrish plant." He asked the Siting Board "to not put Manatee County in the position of being ground zero for an experimental fuel that puts it all on the table when we talk about our quality of life."

"No other state in the country has chosen to introduce this product," Sen. Crist said next. "Why should Florida be the first?"

Thomas Reese, the attorney for ManaSota-88 and Manatee County Save Our Bays, said the Siting Board should disregard all the additional stipulations FPL has offered because "those new conditions are not in the record. The hearing officer never considered them. ...

"The case law says that conditions of certification must be based upon the record and it must be based upon findings of the hearing officer. And the appellate court in its remand stated that you shouldn't be making supplemental findings of fact."

Reese stressed that several of the administrative law judge's findings were now known not to be based on fact - such as his conclusion that gypsum and limestone could not be transported by rail or that the NOx emissions rate was unlikely to get lowered with reburn technology.

A spokeswoman for the Legal Environmental Assistance Foundation shared Reese's assessment. She said LEAF and the National Natural Resource Defense Council filed amicus briefs with the appellate court supporting the Siting Board's denial. She asked the board to "firmly reject Florida Power & Light's last minute efforts to change its project," much of which "directly conflict" with testimony given the administrative law judge. "You're here to explain your decision and not really to make a new one." If FPL wants to revise its project, she said, the Siting Board should tell it "to file a new permit application."

An aquatic biologist with the Save Manatee Club later agreed with that assessment. All of FPL's new information should be included in "a new application" and "let it be exhaustively reviewed."

St. Petersburg City Councilman Lasita reminded the board that his municipality's elected officials passed a resolution opposing Orimulsion. He noted that FPL did not include his community in its service area "Simply put, St. Petersburg, and most of its surrounding neighbors, have virtually nothing to gain and almost everything to lose if this request is approved.. ... This is truly the wrong fuel at the wrong time in the wrong place."

Several residents of the Port Tampa neighborhood spoke in opposition, with a woman noting that when their Civic Association complained about potential truck traffic, FPL, Bitor and Pure Air replied that "trains were absolutely not available ... Every time I turn around, the facts and figures are changing."

A spokeswoman for the Sarasota chapter of the Florida Sierra Club said that the weight of the particulate emissions from Orimulsion is not of as grave concern as the size of the particles, which may be smaller than particulates from oil and "can be inhaled and travel deep into your lungs" to cause "chronic bronchitis, aggravated asthma, acute respiratory symptoms."

"This is a fuel that's not worth the risks," a spokeswoman for the Florida Consumer Action Network testified. "... Saying that Orimulsion solves environmental problems is like saying that smoking cures cancer."

***

During FPL's rebuttal, the president and chief executive of the Chamber of Southwest Florida (a business organization for Lee, Collier, Charlotte, Hendry and Glades counties but not the Tampa Bay area) spoke in favor of the economic benefits of a lower-priced fuel. A Tampa Bay harbor pilot and a retired Coast Guard captain praised the enhanced safety measures for Orimulsion deliveries.

An attorney for FPL encouraged the Siting Board to reverse its decision and include the "new conditions" in an approval. He reminded the panel that "if you do remand (to the administrative law judge), it'll be back here. ... You're going to do this again. Okay? You're going to do this again. And you ought to keep that in mind. It may not be a good Christmas present or Thanksgiving turkey."

In a closing argument, another attorney for FPL described opponents as "sincerely misinformed" and exposed to a "campaign of misinformation and fear mongering. ... A vote for approval is a vote for cleaner air, a safer bay and less expensive power."

During the Siting Board's deliberations, Comptroller Milligan declared that the meeting is not "an evidence gathering forum." He argued that the case, with all the new information, should be remanded back to the administrative law judge for "a formal evidentiary hearing" and that new parties could be allowed to intervene in the proceeding.

Attorney General Butterworth argued that "it is not appropriate to allow so many changes to a proposal" and FPL should instead submit a new application under the Power Plant Siting Act.

A decision to remand the case with new conditions to the administrative law judge and allow "substantially affected parties to intervene" passed 5-2 (Milligan, Mortham, Crawford, Brogan and Chiles in favor with Butterworth and Nelson opposed).

The Orimulsion battle in legal, political and public opinion forums would rage on - with no clear end in sight.

***

Neither FPL nor its opposition got what they wanted from the Siting Board. Yet FPL considered the decision to have Johnston rule on its revised project to be a partial victory, especially since it could feel confident that the judge would be highly likely to accept the additional commitments.

ManaSota-88 intended to argue that Johnston should not accept the remand order and that, if FPL wanted to proceed with an updated plan, it should start fresh with a new permit application that various state agencies could review from scratch. Realizing that strategy could fail, the group prepared legal arguments for yet another prolonged administrative hearing.

Yet, later in the same week as the remand order, the opposition expressed reason for optimism. In Wales, National Power dropped its Orimulsion plans for a closed, 20-year-old plant because the government insisted on a public hearing process similar to what was required of FPL. The Welsh utility decided the costs associated with retrofitting the plant and getting approvals may not be worth the potential benefits.

Meanwhile, Prudential Insurance announced that it reached an undisclosed settlement with PowerGen regarding whether pollution from a plant that used to burn Orimulsion damaged the crops of the company's tenant farmer.

With the loss of National Power, Bitor no longer had clients in the Britain - where Orimulsion made its European debut.

Yet Bitor said it still had prospects elsewhere - including an Illinois Power Company plant at Hennepin, a utility in Brindisi, Italy, and a generating station to be built in Gobo, Japan.

Nor did National Power's decision deter FPL from staying its course.

"We are still committed to our project," a media spokesman for FPL insisted.

***

In its October 1997 newsletter, ManaSota-88 cited a three-year-old document and an anonymous source to claim FPL always intended to switch other power plants besides the units in Parrish to Orimulsion.

The organization referred to the contract with Bitor that FPL submitted to the Public Service Commission in April 1994 when it asked to use some of the potential fuel savings to retrofit the Manatee generating station. Considered proprietary, many details in the document were redacted and blackened out. Yet Rains quoted passages that specifically referred to the 1,600-megawatt Martin plant in Indiantown such as: "In the event FPL's Manatee Units #1 and #2 are converted to use Orimulsion as a primary boiler fuel and subsequently FPL's Martin units #1 or #2, or both, are converted to use Orimulsion as a primary boiler fuel..."

ManaSota-88 also quoted a source who claimed to be a former employee of FPL's fuel management department. The worker was reportedly among 22 of that department's 33 employees who were dismissed in a corporate-wide layoff that removed 2,500 from the utility's payroll.

Prior to 1993, "they were looking at Manatee first because it was not very competitive and was not used a lot," the informant told the Sarasota Herald-Tribune. "Their intent has always been to do Manatee first, then Martin 1 and 2 - then selected 400-megawatt units: Canaveral 1 and 2, Sanford 4 and 5 and Port Everglades 3 and 4." The informant said the chances of converting the Turkey Point plant near the Everglades and Biscayne Bay were "very slim" because of delivery difficulties and proximity to Everglades National Park.

ManaSota-88's source cited personal memory and could provide no documentation that several plants had been considered for conversion to Orimulsion.

FPL responded by saying ManaSota-88 was "taking a giant leap to cause confusion" among the public. It countered that the references to the Martin plant in the Bitor contract were simply to ensure that if it expanded use of the fuel within its system it would get the same low price.

Regarding the anonymous source, FPL said it had "no way of verifying" that the person had been an employee.

***

The televised hearing before Administrative Law Judge Johnston in January 1998 would take on a greater scope and more participants than the proceeding in the same convention center more than two years earlier.

Aside from FPL, the DEP (which recommended approval), Manatee County government (which still officially took "no position" but had a staff attorney present) and Thomas Reese, the lawyer for ManaSota-88 and Manatee Save Our Bays, several other parties now had standing to testify, cross-examine and present evidence: Manatee Citizens Against Pollution (a newly formed group headed by Troxell), CSX Transportation, Ameristeel (an ally of CSX also from Jacksonville and one of FPL's largest corporate customers) and the Civic Association of Port Tampa. The city of St. Petersburg and another new local activist group, the Clean Air Society, asked to add their voices to the opposition.

Early in the hearing witnesses from Air Products and Chemicals and the Pure Air Group testified that they previously presumed ash and gypsum could not be hauled by train but had since learned an unloading station could be built by FPL to transport the waste in special "gondola"-style railcars. The switch from trucks to trains would increase the disposal costs from $3 per ton to $9. Yet FPL and its contractors were willing to alter their previous proposal to alleviate concerns about 202 daily round truck trips on local roads.

Using the same rail line on which products such as coal, phosphate, chlorine and petroleum gas were transported, trains would bring gypsum to a limestone company in the Port Sutton area of Tampa. From there the residue would be shipped by barge across upper Tampa Bay to National Gypsum, a wallboard manufacturer.

Hearing that no railcars or trucks were proposed to go through its neighborhood, the Port Tampa Civic Association withdrew as an intervening party.

The next day, the DEP's top official in charge of the prevention and clean-up of fuel spills would testify - but not on behalf of FPL.

***

Summoned as a witness for ManaSota-88, the chief of the DEP's Bureau of Emergency Response credited FPL and Bitor for the strategy to prevent an Orimulsion spill by using double-hulled tankers, a computerized vessel tracking system and other precautions. Yet she sided with environmentalists' concerns that, if an accident occurred despite those measures, the utility and its supplier would be unlikely to successfully retrieve the emulsified fuel.

Her staff observed the demonstrations in Venezuela that showed a spill that occurred dockside, where booms and other equipment would already be in place, could be contained, she said.

Yet, after they observed another test in the Caribbean Sea, her staff were not convinced a spill could be captured "in open water."

The bureau "unequivocally recommended denial of the permit" to the DEP, she testified. Yet when the DEP recommended approval several months later, it did not mention the contrary opinion of its Emergency Response Bureau.

Reese asked her to authenticate her memo recommending denial.

"Is this still your recommendation?" Reese asked her, referring to the document.

"I have not made a recommendation since then," she responded.

FPL attorneys countered by stressing the bureau chief's positive opinion of the spill prevention strategies. The witness conceded that the precautions were so extensive, a spill in open water could be "highly unlikely" - possibly making the uncertainties of a spill response plan "a moot point."

***

When burning oil with no pollution controls, the Parrish plant emitted 0.3 pounds of nitrogen oxide for every 1 million Btus. Burning Orimulsion without pollution controls would raise that rate to 0.4 pounds.

Consultants for FPL testified that, since the previous administrative hearing, they devised a system that could lower the rate to 0.1255 pounds.

ABB Combustion Services in England designed a system of 24 burners for FPL's boiler that would control the flame temperature and oxygen levels when Orimulsion is ignited. A combustion specialist with the company said those burners should bring the NOx rate down to 0.24 pounds.

A representative of Environmental Energy Research testified that the California company designed a set of fuel injectors to be installed higher in the boiler. The higher flame would burn off some of the escaping gas while generating about 23 percent of the heat needed for the boiler. He claimed the "reburn technology" could lower the 0.24 pounds rate achieved by the low-NOx burners to 0.1255.

Yet the vendors, who "guaranteed" the lower

emissions that they cited, acknowledged that some information about their systems must be regarded as protected trade secrets and would remain "confidential."

Reese argued that those details should be made public so other experts could determine whether the lower NOx emissions being promised were indeed possible.

FPL attorneys objected.

"I don't see why you need to create a problem," Judge Johnston told Reese as he ruled in FPL's favor. "I don't see the relevance of your inquiry."

Manatee Citizens Against Pollution challenged FPL's contention that NOx levels would not exceed the "actual historical" level of 7,318 tons annually.

FPL based that figure on 1993 and 1994 data collected before it filed its Orimulsion application.

MCAP noted that, in 1995, NOx emissions at Parrish totaled 5,598 tons and, in 1996, dropped to 4,913 tons. It argued that those years should be used to calculate "historical" emissions not to be exceeded.

FPL's engineering manager for the Orimulsion project said 1995 and 1996 were atypical years during which economics, weather and "unscheduled outages (lasting) over 30 days" caused the Parrish plant to be underutilized. He said the 7,318 tons figure "falls within a typical range."

MCAP countered that, in September 1994, FPL installed "steam atomizers" at its Parrish plant that mix steam with fuel at the tip of a burner. Fuel is "atomized" into finer particles that burn more efficiently, requiring less oxygen for combustion. MCAP posed the possibility that the new equipment caused the lower NOx rates.

The FPL witness agreed that steam atomizers "improve the combustion process" but disagreed that the new equipment would be "very effective in reducing NOx."

The environmental groups challenged the accuracy of the calculation that 7,318 tons annually should be the permitted maximum for NOx because FPL based the figure on 1993 and 1994 data. FPL did not install "continuous emission monitors," which precisely measure the weight of pollutants emitted by the hour, day, month and year, until required by the federal Clean Air Act of 1995.

Yet an environmental engineer who worked as a consultant for FPL said how many tons of various pollutants came from the Parrish smokestacks could be accurately determined with old-fashioned arithmetic. Taking the total amount of oil burned and the amount of heat that oil would produce in the Parrish plant's burners, the witness said he could determine the expected emissions of each pollutant. He said he could personally confirm that, after the switch to Orimulsion, annual NOx emissions could be kept at 7,318 tons and particulates would not exceed 858 tons, half of what was quoted in the 1995 hearing.

***

The former chief of the U.S. Coast Guard's Marine Protection Division, who shared his findings with the Siting Board more than four months previously, testified that a statistical chance of one spill could occur for every 10,000 FPL oil deliveries at Port Manatee. Yet he concluded that, because of the stricter shipping precautions to be taken by FPL and Bitor, the probability of an Orimulsion spill would be one in 100,000 shipments.

If a spill of the oil substitute did occur, he felt confident that "the majority" of the emulsified bitumen could be recovered. By comparison, he said, a 20 percent recovery rate for an oil spill is considered "successful."

The marine biologist from the University of Miami, who had also appeared before the Siting Board, testified that, under laboratory conditions, he tested how Orimulsion spilled in sea water affected scallops, anchovies, blue crabs and 17 other species - paying special attention to the larvae of sea trout, "the most sensitive life stage of the most sensitive species."

He said his tests were a worst-case scenario because he presumed no recovery efforts would be conducted and that all of the bitumen remained in the bay for up to 10 weeks. He also noted that, in the tank tests, there could be "no active avoidance" of the dispersed fuel by fish - which would occur in an actual spill in the bay.

He concluded that, in the worst-case scenario, 8.4 percent of Tampa Bay's marine life could die because of an Orimulsion spill. Yet he felt certain that the bay's fish and shellfish would experience "total recovery in less than two years" and damage to the bay "would not be considered ecologically significant."

Regarding sea life in shallow waters, the researcher said a wind-driven oil slick would probably be more harmful than an Orimulsion spill driven by tidal currents.

A veterinarian and toxicologist testified on behalf of FPL that she dipped dead turkeys up to 15 times in a child's swimming pool filled with salt water and Orimulsion. The bitumen failed to coat the birds as oil would and instead had "a peppering effect." She said the black specks were only on the outer feathers and were easily removed with olive oil.

When cross-examined, the witnesses dismissed concerns about the additive phenol and studies indicating it causes "gender-bending" deformities in fish and wildlife. They stressed the prior research concerned long-term exposure to the surfactant, not the brief exposure to a dissipating amount from an Orimulsion spill.

Another FPL witness, a petroleum chemist from the University of Massachusetts at Amherst, testified that nonylphenol ethoxylate must be in an environment deprived of oxygen to break down into phenol. His lab tests reportedly showed Intan-100, the brand of emulsifier in Orimulsion, would take 30 to 45 days of exposure to sunlight and other natural elements after a spill "to completely break down" into carbon dioxide and water. He described the bitumen in the emulsified fuel to be more "weathered" - or aged by the Earth - than oil and said it would not decompose into the highly toxic compounds that occur with an oil spill at sea.

Several days later, Manatee Citizens Against Pollution arranged for a biochemist with the British environmental group Friends of the Earth to challenge those findings.

The witness cited a study indicating that phenol exposure caused sexual deformities in young male rainbow trout. He noted that sunlight barely penetrates the surface waters of Tampa Bay and will be of scant help in getting phenol to biograde quickly. He stressed that the bay has oxygen-low areas where phenol could accumulate, such as mangrove-fringed shorelines. "That's why mangroves have those little roots going up, to get some air."

He regarded eggs and other young life as the most endangered. The chemical will "bio-accumulate" in fish and shellfish and then in "any creatures feeding on them, such as wading birds."

Several days later, MCAP arranged a telephone conference call with an environmental consultant and former general manager of Friends of the Earth, who testified that particulates - specks of ash and other particles - from Orimulsion are "significantly smaller" than those of oil. He argued that the smaller particulates stay in the lungs and cause disease.

An attorney for FPL countered that particulates from burned Orimulsion can be "breathed back out more readily because of their small size."

***

St. Petersburg City Councilman Lasita and an assistant city attorney addressed the spill issue. They presented that municipality's resolution against the Orimulsion project and expressed concerns about the possible negative impacts of a tanker spill on their coastal community.

***

Throughout the hearing, Reese said he wanted to make the case that natural gas, delivered by pipeline instead of tanker and emitting less air pollutants than oil or Orimulsion, should be the preferred fuel for the Parrish plant.

Yet FPL continued to counter that natural gas would not be a viable option for its Manatee County operation and that Orimulsion would provide more diversity for its entire system's "fuel mix."

The utility's lead attorney told Johnston that the "remand order" from the governor and Cabinet did not instruct him to consider natural gas and turn the permit hearing "into a case about a third fuel."

***

On behalf of FPL, the DEP administrator in charge of processing applications under the Power Plant Siting Act testified that the agency recommended approval of the utility's previous as well as revised Orimulsion plans.

He called reduced levels of NOx and particulate pollution in the updated plan as "achievable." He added that the state's environmental agency supported the new conditions regarding fuel shipments and the switch from trucks to railcars for transportation of pollution control residue.

An economist testified on behalf of FPL that, if Orimulsion started replacing oil as of 2000, FPL's customers statewide could see the "fuel costs" portions of their bills drop by $18.9 million. Government institutions, such as public schools, reportedly would save $1.3 million on electric bills that year.

By 2019, the final year in FPL's 20-year contract, consumer savings (in 1998 dollars) could total $374 million, with taxpayer-supported institutions sharing $7.7 million of that total, the economist continued.

He added that, including temporary construction work to retrofit the plant, FPL's project could create 374 jobs and add 359 jobs to the regional economy. Factoring in extra property taxes, promised donations to a trust fund for Tampa Bay and other benefits, the Orimulsion project could be a $2 million annual boost for Manatee County's economy and a $7.2 million positive impact for the bay region.

Yet the economist acknowledged that he based his analysis on "forecasts" about fuel prices provided by FPL.

FPL projected that, in 2000, the cost of generating 1 million Btus of heat in its steam generating plants with oil would be $2.96; for natural gas, $2.73; for coal, $1.75; and for Orimulsion, $1.74.

FPL projected that, by 2019, those prices would be $7.59 for oil, $6.44 for natural gas, $2.58 for coal and $2.55 for Orimulsion.

The Clean Air Society countered that FPL had been known to overestimate fuel prices.

Reese, the ManaSota-88 attorney, said the analysis failed to presume that the oil industry could price its product more competitively if Orimulsion were allowed in the United States. "They're not going to let a fuel like Orimulsion come in and take their market away for 20 years."

Opposition groups asked FPL's economist if the consumer savings were "guaranteed."

"It's not so much a guarantee," the witness said of FPL's contract to buy Orimulsion at a price tied to what the Jacksonville Electric Authority paid for coal. "It's an insurance policy. We can lock in a long-term, low-cost fuel. ... If you can find anyone who will guarantee any (economic) forecast, I'd like to meet him."

***

On Jan. 26, Johnston devoted several hours to the general public portion of the public hearing - allowing citizens not personally affiliated with FPL or any of the intervening parties to speak for up to five minutes each.

Senator Crist from St. Petersburg expressed his concerns about a potential spill, noting that he represented a district spanning parts of Pinellas and Hillsborough counties and "a lot of the bay in between."

The conservation chairman of the National Sierra Club came from San Francisco to challenge the results of mock spill tests that did not mimic the effects of wind and tide. "Tampa Bay is not contained in beakers and vials," he said.

The Florida president of the Izaak Walton League said pollution risks could jeopardize Manatee County's most prominent industries, agriculture and tourism.

The Florida Consumer Action Network unscrolled a petition from almost 5,000 Floridians opposed to FPL's plan.

Although outnumbered, several citizens spoke in favor - including the Coast Guard captain in charge of marine safety for Tampa Bay, who said the updated spill prevention plan consisted of "worldwide best practices."

A resident who founded the pro-Orimulsion group Manatee Citizens for Clean Air and Water said area environmentalists should instead be focusing their ire on Tampa Electric Co.'s coal-burning plant in neighboring Hillsborough County. "Who's the one fouling our air and water?"

A 14-year-old boy from Hernando County wanted to submit his prize-winning school science project. He said he intended to prove his hypothesis that Orimulsion would be more damaging to salt water plants than oil. Using a sample of Orimulsion his father obtained from Florida State University, the boy said he discovered that his hypothesis was wrong and Orimulsion would be no more damaging than oil and could be recovered at the same 25 percent rate.

"I care about the environment," he testified. "I get really mad when people appeal to the emotions and not the facts."

***

When an executive from FPL's Power Generation Division testified, the environmental groups challenged the potential consumer savings.

Troxell noted that the utility initially said the potential savings for a typical household would likely be $3.50 a month. Yet an FPL cost analysis filed before the hearing indicated a new working estimate of less than a third of a cent per kilowatt hour, meaning that a household using 1,000 kilowatt hours monthly would instead save $3.10 on the fuel portion of its bill.

Troxell wanted to know when customers could expect their monthly savings.

Having acknowledged that the utility was just 40 percent finished with its engineering and still revising figures, C.O. Woody, the division president, said the capital costs for retrofitting the plant would be paid first and consumers "will not realize full savings until approximately two years after the conversion is done."

Quoting figures FPL presented the previous week, Troxell said the utility expected the increased demand for electricity to average 1.87 percent annually over the next 20 years.

"According to your annual report to stockholders, it (load growth) exceeds 3 percent," Troxell told the executive, stressing that the fuel savings would be spread among more ratepayers during each passing year.

***

A fuel price forecaster and an air emissions specialist hired by CSX Transportation both challenged FPL's claim the switch to Orimulsion would result in more than $1 billion in consumer savings ($3.8 billion when adjusted for inflation) over 20 years.

CSX officials said the railroad spends $300,000 annually on electricity bills and stepped into the legal fight with FPL to represent the ratepayers' best interest.

Testifying for CSX, the president of Energy Ventures Analysis of Arlington, Virginia, said he conducted a "bottoms-up analysis" of the Orimulsion project. He called FPL's consumer savings projections "wildly optimistic."

The witness claimed the conversion would likely be awash in $65 million in red ink after 10 years and, in 20 years, be just $11 million ahead of expenses. "Taking on a $379 million project for an $11 million benefit that doesn't come until the year 2019 is not a good investment," he said when summarizing his testimony after the hearing.

He agreed with FPL's projection that oil

prices would escalate but not as dramatically as proposed. Although FPL predicted oil would cost $5.07 for every 1 million British thermal units in 2010, the witness predicted a price of $3.20. Considering the use of coal-fired plants in Florida burning a fuel priced like Orimulsion, the energy consultant said the plant would more likely be used at 73 to 74 percent of capacity and not "displace" as much other fuel in the FPL system. He speculated that because of the efficiency with which it burns and the need for less pollution controls, natural gas could become a cheaper alternative.

An atmospheric scientist with RTP Environmental Associates of Green Brook, New Jersey, testified that, when burning Orimulsion, the Parrish plant would emit far more pollution than FPL expected - possibly triggering a "prevention of significant deterioration" review and special permitting requirements under federal law. He presented calculations that, rather that 7,318 tons annually, the "actual historical" emissions of NOx were from 5,478 and 6,813 tons because of additions installed to the burners in 1995. He also contended that the "actual historical" emissions of particulates should be 813 tons annually and that, because of numerous factors FPL failed to consider, will rise to 1,112 tons.

CSX's ally, AmeriSteel Corp., next called for

an array of written guarantees from FPL to protect ratepayers. The vice-president of the manufacturer and recycler of steel products testified that, as FPL's largest single-meter customer, AmeriSteel spends $12.4 million annually for electricity and had a hefty stake in the case's outcome.

To continue doing business in Florida, AmeriSteel expressed concerns about rising expenses. The company claimed that energy costs at its two mills in Tennessee were 70 percent less and for its South Carolina mill 25 percent less than what it paid in Florida.

AmeriSteel wanted FPL to sign a commitment that ratepayers will receive "a minimum guaranteed savings"; ratepayers will be "held harmless and must not bear any future costs associated with any environmental clean-up"; "all expenses associated with media campaigns, lobbying activities and similar spending associated with seeking approval of the plan must be borne by FPL rather than ratepayers"; FPL must submit an annual "cost-benefit analysis" to the Siting Board; and, if FPL receives any fees or royalties from contractors whose pollution controls include "trade secrets," that income should benefit consumers through lower rates.

The next week, FPL summoned a surprise rebuttal witness to discredit the fuel-cost forecaster who testified for its corporate opponents. The economist from Massachusetts published a monthly report about crude oil prices, wrote articles and books about oil markets and testified in government hearings about oil cartels and related issues.

The witness based his methodology on trends set by stock market investors. He said the previous forecaster failed to consider the likelihood of "disruptions" in the Middle East, Saudi Arabia's tendency to limit production to get global prices up and the North Sea's history of producing less oil than anticipated. He preferred to rely on the BP Royalty Trust, a stock paying "a dividend linked to the price of oil." Pension funds, mutual funds and private investors bought the stock and received an interest in the daily production of oil by BP Exploration at Prudhoe Bay, Alaska. He contended the stock reflected "the market expectation of the rise in future oil prices."

If the previous forecaster's assumptions were applied retroactively, the stock price of BP Royalty Trust would be a third of the latest quote, FPL's witness stressed.

Reese, attorney for two of the environmental groups, called the methodology being cited as "pure speculation" because it was based on what stock investors may or may not do. "We might as well take a roulette wheel and spin it around."

Yet FPL remained adamant that oil prices

were likely to far exceed that of coal and Orimulsion in the future and that CSX's motives in trying to block a less expensive oil substitute from the market were based in protecting its coal-hauling business.

***

After more than 100 hours of testimony and the presentations of a plethora of exhibits, FPL and the intervening parties that remained presented closing arguments.

Johnston allowed FPL to recall several witnesses for its rebuttal. One by one, executives and consultants defended their earlier stances about pollution data, spill prevention, fuel costs and other points of dispute. In doing so, they referred to their opposition's witnesses as "truly inexperienced" and to their comments as "nonsense," "premature" and a "misrepresentation" of scientific fact.

"The weight of the evidence is on our side," FPL's lead attorney concluded.

Reese and attorneys for CSX could not persuade Johnston to let their witnesses return and respond to FPL's rebuttal. Yet Johnston agreed to accept any counterarguments in writing, which he received a few weeks later. (In his written response, the biologist and chemist from Friends of the Earth who testified for MCAP accused FPL witnesses who debunked his findings about phenol of a "preference for personal insults rather than sound science.")

Regardless of what Johnston would think of their case, the opponents succeeded in their strategy to get all of their legal and technical challenges on the record. They could then quote from that record before a higher authority.

Before parting, lawyers for FPL and its opposition shook hands and complimented each other's efforts - knowing they were to spar again before the Siting Board.

***

In early March, the Orimulsion debate ignited again in an unexpected location - Palmetto High School in Manatee County.

A science teacher at the public school arranged for a presentation about the controversial project by FPL's area manager, one of the utility's staff environmental experts and a former biologist.

A parent of two students heard about the upcoming presentation and notified Troxell. The founder of MCAP called a School Board member, who contacted the principal. The principal agreed to let the parent and Troxell attend the assembly the next morning.

Afterward, Troxell and the parent told the administration that they wanted equal time.

The principal agreed to arrange another forum the next week so they could convey arguments against the fuel change to the same students. "We'll have a point-counterpoint. It can be a springboard for a good discussion in the classroom."

***

Almost 10 months before the deadline Denmark set for Venezuela to replace phenol in Orimulsion or lose SK Power as a client, Bitor America confirmed that researchers found a new emulsifying additive. Yet, contending that the original formula is environmentally safe, the distributor said FPL would still receive Orimulsion with phenol instead of what Bitor Europe would offer to its Danish client.

The decision to change its product for a European customer but not FPL angered MCAP founder Troxell and others in Florida. Troxell wanted to know details about the replacement surfactant. He contended that Venezuela's alteration of the original formula implied that the mixture with phenol must be flawed.

Yet Bitor America declined to release specifics because of "commercial and competitive" reasons, stating that tests remained in "the pilot stage" and Danish authorities had yet to give their consent.

The secrecy did not surprise Rains of ManaSota-88. "Their idea of proprietary information is sadly askew," she said of FPL and Bitor. "Anything they don't want someone to investigate, they stamp it 'proprietary.'"

With the administrative hearing over and Johnston's opinion still pending, Orimulsion's opponents doubted information about a new and perhaps improved additive could be entered into the record. Yet that did not mean they would have to be silent about the latest revelation.

"It certainly is going to be brought up before the governor and Cabinet," Troxell vowed.

***

On April 17, more than two months after closing arguments, Johnston released his ruling based on 2,958 pages of testimony, a mountain of exhibits and 351 "findings of fact." He again recommended approval of FPL's use of Orimulsion.

"The additional evidence admitted at the remand hearing supports the fundamental conclusion" that the conversion project "meets the criteria" for a new power plant in state law, Johnston concluded.

"He clearly considered and weighed the evidence," FPL's lead attorney said of Johnston. "This is a very careful and wise judge. He picked up on the nuances and subtleties."

The president of Bitor America commended the judge for a "thorough review and analysis of a tremendous amount of data and information."

Yet the opposition groups felt Johnston to have been biased.

"Whenever we made a point, he found some way to excuse it," Reese said. "We have a lot of points to argue before the governor and Cabinet, a lot of debatable points."

"The recommendation raises more questions than it answers," a media spokesman for CSX said. "The governor and the Cabinet should be hard pressed to approve it."

Five years had passed since Manatee County residents initially heard of Orimulsion and how it might alter their quality of life, for better or for worse. Under FPL's original timetable, the Parrish plant would have been retrofitted and tankers would have been unloading Orimulsion at Port Manatee by this time. If the Power Plant Siting Board approved FPL's revised plan, the renovations could begin that summer and the plant could be burning Orimulsion in 2000.

With Johnston's endorsement of its additional concessions, FPL needed to convince just one of the four members of the Siting Board who voted for denial to change his mind and its switch to Orimulsion would be underway.

***

In the weeks prior to the June 24 Siting Board hearing, the pro and anti factions strived to strengthen their cases and endorsements.

State Senator John McKay, a Republican from Manatee County running for re-election in the fall, shifted from being undecided to joining State Rep. Mark Ogles of Manatee and State Rep. Lisa Carlton of Sarasota County, both of whom opposed the Orimulsion project prior to the 1996 Siting Board hearing.

"There remain too many unanswered questions relative to the potential health hazards and the possible catastrophic spills from this experimental fuel," McKay wrote Chiles and the Cabinet. "... Given the apparently overwhelming opposition to Orimulsion, it is our duty to listen to the people. If we are to make unpopular decisions, we should do so based upon factual data which is sorely lacking in this instance."

State Sen. Katherine Harris, a Republican from Sarasota County running against incumbent Secretary of State Mortham, launched a television campaign commercial attacking the incumbent for voting in favor of Orimulsion in 1996.

Yet the narrow majority on the Manatee County Commission still insisted on remaining neutral.

***

On June 24, before another overflow crowd, the Siting Board convened to hear FPL make its updated case.

FPL President Paul Evanson emphasized that Administrative Law Judge Johnston determined "that the additional information only strengthened his original conclusion that this project should be approved." The conversion to Orimulsion at Parrish would generate "almost three times the amount of power with less pollution than there is today" while providing "lower electric bills for half the state of Florida." Despite environmentalists' preference for it, Evanson emphasized that "converting to gas is simply not an option at Manatee." He urged the elected officials to base their decision "on the record and not on some of the rhetoric."

The utility's lead attorney stressed that the additional conditions are "more stringent limits... This project is an air quality regulator's dream come true," the lawyer said. "... All of the many agencies that reviewed this project over the past four years have concluded that it meets the standards that they have set to protect public health and welfare. No agency, including Manatee County, has taken a contrary position. ... it's time to let FPL off the permitting treadmill."

A Coast Guard spokesman, an executive vice-president of Petroleos de Venezuela, a weekly newspaper publisher from Longboat Key, the president and business manager of International Brotherhood of Electrical Workers Local Union 820 and others spoke in favor of FPL's application.

As the first speaker in opposition, Reese, the attorney for ManaSota-88 and Manatee Save Our Bays, emphasized that Orimulsion is a high-sulfur fuel. If the Siting Board "had the same proposal here today to burn coal that was 2.9 percent sulfur, we'd have the same position. You should not be burning high-sulfur fuel."

An attorney for CSX said that, before the Public Service Commission, FPL spoke of customer savings of $6 billion over 20 years. By the first administrative hearing, that estimate reportedly dropped to $3.8 billion and, at the remand hearing, to $717 million. He said those savings could be "further reduced if the capacity factor of 87 percent is not sustainable."

About two dozen more speakers expressed their objections including State Sen. Harris of Sarasota (Mortham's election opponent), State Sen. Crist of St. Petersburg, Mayor David Fischer and Councilman Lasita of St. Petersburg, the vice mayor of South Pasadena (also a municipality in Pinellas County), Manatee County Commissioners Stein, McClash and Bruce, and representatives from the Florida Wildlife Federation, Florida Audubon Society, Brotherhood of Locomotive Engineers, United Transportation Union Local 1035, Florida Consumer Action Network (which presented 15,000 petitions), National Sierra Club and its Florida chapter and other groups.

In rebuttal, FPL's attorney insisted the utility resolved its opponents' criticisms about potential spills and air pollution. He urged the Siting Board to "please base your decision on the facts. I think if you do, you have to conclude that this project meets every test. And compared to oil, Orimulsion will give us cleaner air, a safer bay, lower electric bills."

Gov. Chiles opened the matter for discussion among the Cabinet members.

Without getting into details, Attorney General Butterworth made a motion to approve a draft order for denial prepared two days earlier by the general counsel of the Governor's Office and Cabinet members' staffs.

Education Commissioner Brogan seconded Butterworth's motion after commending the presentations of FPL and its challengers but adding that "it still troubles me deeply that Venezuela, which provides this alternative fuel source to so many others, doesn't employ it itself in its own borders."

Secretary of State Mortham made the most extensive remarks:

"Governor, this may be the toughest issue that certainly I have contemplated since being on this Cabinet - other than clemency. ... And the vote that I cast today will not be cast lightly or without hours of thought, contemplation and prayer. ... And my thinking on this issue has really boiled down to this: While the facts seem to support the application, the people don't. In fact, it scares them to death. Letters and phone calls to my office have been 100 to 1 against the use of this fuel." Mortham added that, being elected, Cabinet members are "the voice of the people." In that capacity, "I intend to vote for the citizens that have spoken loud and clear and against this application."

In a roll call vote, Mortham and Brogan changed their previous positions in favor of FPL and joined Chiles, Butterworth, Insurance Commissioner Nelson and Comptroller Milligan in approving an order of denial. Only Agriculture Commissioner Crawford, who did not say why, stuck with his stance in support of the fuel conversion project.

In a 6-1 decision, Florida's highest ranking elected officials refused to let Orimulsion be introduced into their state.

FPL would have to weigh whether to accept a costly loss or continue the fuel fight with another court appeal. More than a month would pass before factions on both sides of the issue would learn what would or would not happen next.

***

On July 30, FPL President Evanson and Woody, its executive in charge of power generation, came to Manatee County to confer with local employees and make a public announcement.

The utility would not appeal the Siting Board's denial, they told media.

"It is now time to put the proposal to burn Orimulsion behind us," Evanson said in a prepared statement.

He and Woody were unsure how much FPL spent on its effort to import and burn the hybrid fuel since it first tested Orimulsion at its Sanford plant but acknowledged that the sum would be "in the millions."

The executives remained convinced that the facts proved Orimulsion made economic and environmental sense but that Chiles and the Cabinet succumbed to political pressure.

Juan Pulgar, president of Bitor America, shared that bitter sentiment. "Frankly, the governor and the Cabinet managed to turn a win-win project into a lose-lose cop-out."

Yet those on the prevailing side regarded FPL's obituary for its Orimulsion project as evidence that a determined, relentless grass-roots movement can succeed, even when taking on a corporate titan.

"People can make a difference," Rains of ManaSota-88 said.

A lingering uncertainty remained, however: What would eventually become of the oil-burning Parrish plant? Would FPL continue to operate it at a third of its capacity or, to meet an increasing demand for power, maximize its use as well as its air pollution emissions? Or could another outcome of Florida's five-year fuel fight be possible?

***

Several months later, in April 1999, Houston-based Coastal Corp., a publicly held company that built, owned and operated more than 18,000 miles of natural gas pipelines, announced plans for a new pipeline to extend from Mobile Bay, Alabama, across the Gulf of Mexico to Florida, making landfall in the general vicinity south of Tampa Bay.

Gradually, the route of the Gulfstream Natural Gas System took shape. After being submerged across more than 450 miles of the Gulf, the $1.6 billion pipeline would enter Florida at Port Manatee, where the County Commission unanimously and enthusiastically welcomed Gulfstream as a new tenant. A 100-foot-wide easement would bring the underground, 36-inch diameter pipeline across 294 miles of the Florida peninsula stretching eastward across Manatee County into Hardee County, with a northern spur in Polk and Osceola counties, and continuing east into Highlands County and south into Okeechobee, Martin and Palm Beach counties.

As it crossed Manatee County, the future pipeline would pass the front gate of FPL's Parrish generating station.

***

In February 2001, the Federal Energy Regulatory Commission authorized a permit for

Gulfstream, which Coastal sold to a new partnership formed by Williams Inc., a gas exploration company, and Duke Energy.

No longer able to claim that natural gas would not be a viable option for the Parrish plant, FPL, having dropped its preference for a new fuel from a foreign supplier, opted for a cleaner alternative from a domestic source benefiting American workers.

The utility converted the generating station so that it could burn either oil or gas, whichever would be less expensive. "But, to the extent we can make use of natural gas, there will be improved environmental performance and lower air emissions," an FPL spokesperson said after the state DEP approved the renovation in the summer of 2002.

FPL also applied to build a separate, $560 million, 1,100-megawatt gas-fired generator on its Parrish property with all the pollution controls required of new power plants. The additional unit would increase the number of customers served by the Manatee facility from 340,000 to 575,000.

Although MCAP and others expressed concerns that both plants could possibly be operated simultaneously at maximum capacity, a hearing before Administrative Law Judge Charles Stampelos lacked the acrimony of the previous proceedings before Judge Johnston.

In September 2003, Stampelos recommended approval of the gas-fired plant to the new Siting Board chaired by Gov. Jeb Bush. By the next summer, the new facility would be under construction.

Prior to the renewal of the air pollution permit for the existing plant, FPL told the Manatee County Commission it would "voluntarily" install "reburn technology" at the 27-year-old facility to further reduce NOx emissions.

Environmentalists wanted a "guarantee" that the older plant would continue to be used only at a fraction of its capacity.

Yet the county commissioners acknowledged that no such guarantee could be given because FPL would be legally obligated to provide electricity to its customers if it had power available.

After installation of reburn technology on one of the older plant's boilers in late 2005, FPL reported a 16.5 percent decline in NOx and noted that a total drop in the smog-causing pollutant could be closer to 40 percent when the emissions control system got added to the second boiler.

Yet more change for the Parrish plant and FPL's statewide "energy mix" would still be ahead.

***

In 2009, FPL announced plans to erect solar panels on about 500 acres of its 9,500-acre facility in Manatee. The additional energy source would be expected to generate 75 megawatts of electricity for as many as 17,000 homes.

On Dec. 31, 2016, the Manatee Solar Energy Center came online. FPL's new Citrus Solar Energy Center in DeSoto County, Babcock Ranch Solar Energy Center in Charlotte County and the Manatee Solar Energy Center would collectively generate 225 of FPL's 335 megawatts of solar energy to keep the lights on and refrigerators humming for 60,000 of the utility's 4.9 million customers.

Each of the new solar centers cost $130 million, a clear indication that the cost of going solar was dropping. Eight years earlier, the company spent $100 million on its first solar plant, which generates 25 megawatts.

At a February 2017 celebration during which school children from seven counties and invited guests could see the Manatee Solar Energy Center, FPL President and CEO Eric Silagy announced plans for eight more solar plants with a total capacity of 600 megawatts, enough electricity for 120,000 homes.

"We're farming the sun," a media spokeswoman for the utility proclaimed.

In 2021, the FPL Manatee Energy Storage Center, a battery installation charged by the FPL Manatee Solar Energy Center, would extend the benefits of "farming the sun" by providing power even during hours without sunlight.

By then, FPL boasted operations of 41 solar energy centers across the state with plans for many more.

Sustainable energy advocates would heavily criticize FPL and other Florida utilities for attempting to limit what they regarded as a competitor, the residential rooftop solar industry. Yet they acknowledged FPL's growing commitment to solar for its grid.

Between 2020 and 2023, FPL would add five more solar energy centers at scattered rural locations in Manatee County.

The utility expected that, by the end of the decade, nearly 40 percent of its power would be generated by zero-emissions sources.

***

In 2006, after several years of losing clients, Venezuela ceased production of Orimulsion. Its last shipment of the controversial blended fuel went to China in March 2007.

***

About the author

Dale Andrew White's journalism has appeared in the Sarasota Herald-Tribune, St. Petersburg Times, Miami Herald, Orlando Sentinel, Florida Times-Union, Gainesville Sun, Florida Living and several other publications. He and three other staff writers for GateHouse Media were nominated for the Pulitzer Prize for explanatory reporting for "Rising Seas," a newspaper series about the effects of climate change on coastal Florida. His non-fiction books include "Encounters with Authors," a collection of interviews, and "A Florida Anthology," a collection about Florida history.